The only book you need to master office politics.

The Unwritten Laws Of Office politics

By - Jimson Rk.

Copyright© 2026 Jimson Rk. All rights are reserved by the author. No part of this publication may be reproduced, distributed, or transmitted in any form or by any means, including photocopying, recording, or other electronic or mechanical methods without the prior written permission of the author.

Paperback ISBN - 978-93-5773-241-3

Hardback ISBN - 978-93-5782-410-1

Author Information:

Email: jimsonrk@gmail
Linkedin @jimson rk
Personal Instagram @Jimson rk

A note From Author

If a company is toxic for you, walk away before it starts dulling your creativity and killing your motivation. You don't own the company, and you don't owe it your peace. Sustaining in a toxic workplace is no less than drinking poison slowly; you are trading your mental health for a paycheck, creativity for conformity, knowledge for subservience, and personal life for an illusion of security.

Don't try to fix a culture that feeds on manipulation or play a game designed to exhaust you—you'll lose more than you gain. Your worth is more than you can imagine, and your talents are more needed in a good environment. Remember, the longer you adapt to dysfunction, the more it convinces you that suffering is normal. That's how toxic systems win; not by strength, but by silent endurance.

Loyalty is beautiful, but not when it becomes self-destruction. You were hired to add value, not to sacrifice your mental health.

Walk away before the place that pays your bills ends up billing your soul.

Contents

Master the art of storytelling...................... 27 - 32

Don't let loyalty blind you..........................33 - 38

Play Dumb to Obtain Power....................... 39 - 50

The promotion playbook .... 51 - 60

Build your reputation to obtain recognition ...... 61 - 70

Build your brand to obtain authority .... 71 – 78

Learn the art of argument .... 79 - 90

The Power of Respectful Disagreement .... 91 - 102

A smile can hide the deepest betrayal .... 103 - 112

The hidden hand behind power .... 113 - 120

Bonus

Bonus – 1 .... 123 - 124

Bonus – 2 .... 125 - 128

Bonus – 3 .... 129 - 132

Bonus – 4 .... 133 - 134

Bonus – 5 .... 135 - 138

Bonus – 6 .... 139 - 142

Bonus – 7 .... 143 - 148

Bonus – 8 .... 149 - 156

Bonus – 9 .... 157 - 160

Bonus – 10 .... 161 - 166

PREFACE

Learn to identify fake friends

Not everyone who laughs with you is loyal, and not every hand offered in kindness is free of strings. Some people approach you not to support you but to use your progress for their own benefit.

Fake friends linger close. They observe your moves, study your rise, and exploit each open space in your life while wearing a mask of concern. They may listen or offer advice, even show comfort, yet their loyalty carries a price. It stays only when your success feeds their motive.

They'll nod, agree, and praise your ideas, yet every compliment can carry a hidden motive. They feed on trust, twist conversations, and quietly measure how much influence they can claim without being noticed.

Recognizing them isn't about paranoia—it's about clarity. Notice who vanishes when challenges arise, who envies your victories rather than celebrates them, and who subtly chips away at your confidence while smiling to your face. Protect your inner circle. True friendship strengthens; fake friendship drains and your peace is worth safeguarding.

Fake friends can feel closer than true ones. They offer comfort, show kindness, and stand by you, but only until their purpose is served. Then you would find yourself drained, while they walked away unnoticed.

Learn how to be loyal

Loyalty can look noble on the surface, yet in the corporate world, it's often a leash disguised as praise. You're urged to stay committed, wait your turn, give more than your role requires, while the system studies how far you can stretch before you reach a breaking point.

In truth, loyalty doesn't protect you—it binds you. The longer you remain unquestioning, the easier it is for them to shape your role to their needs, shifting you from place to place under the label of teamwork, and then discard you the moment your value fades.

So choose loyalty that serves your growth. Hold to your principles, not their slogans. A company drops people the moment they stop serving its targets, while those who stayed loyal walk out with nothing except exhaustion.

Learn how to build your brand

How do you want the world to read you? A friend sees one version, a boss sees another, yet both respond to the image you carry. What you project often speaks louder than your truth.

Your skill matters, your effort matters, yet inside the office they rise only when people notice them. Visibility becomes currency. Those who understand this move faster, not because they are better, but because they refuse to stay unseen.

You can do everything right and still fade behind someone who understands the art of being read. When your intent stays hidden, your contribution becomes easy to ignore.

So craft your presence with care. Let perception reflect your depth rather than shadow it. When you shape the story others hold about you, you shape the future you step into.

You are not promoted for what is true, but for what is perceived. Learn to shape the story, and you shape your future.

Learn how to tell your story

Imagine you are a husband, and your wife is sick; lying in bed while you prepare a bowl of soup and bring it to her.

Now, you offer it to her in one of these two ways:

(a) *"Here's the soup. Drink it."* You place it on the table and leave the room.

(b) *"My love, I made this soup to help you feel better. While reading about your condition on internet, I found that the mushrooms in it can boost your immune system, give you strength, and ease some of your symptoms. Drink this and get some rest. Don't worry about the housework—I'll take care of it. If you need anything else, I'll be in the kitchen."*

Both brought the same bowl and walked out the same door, yet one did it as a task, while the other infused the act with care, intention, and a quiet story of healing and support. It is in this difference that the heart reacts.

Clearly, the wife would be more moved not by the soup itself, but by the story that came with it. The way you frame your intent can transform an ordinary act into an experience that heals, connects, and stays remembered. That's the power of storytelling; it turns gestures into emotions, actions into meaning, and simple moments into something people feel deeply. You're not just telling a story; you're shaping how the world receives you.

Learn how to build Align

A sharp mind alone can impress, but without a network, it achieves little. A polished gun may look powerful, but without a bullet, it's just metal shining in vain. Similarly, in the office, your skills and ideas remain powerless unless you have people willing to notice, support, and amplify them.

Your work matters, but the crucial question is: who sees it, and who understands your contribution? Work is like the brain of our body-essential, yet useless without the rest of our body part. In the same way, your contributions are valuable for your career only if they are recognized; otherwise, they risk becoming shadows in someone else's story.

Therefore, forge alignments carefully. Choose colleagues who act with integrity and value mutual growth, not just personal gain. Without the right network, even your sharpest moves can leave you exposed, isolated, and overlooked.

Learn to Take Credit for Your Work

In the game of influence, credit is the hidden currency of promotion. You may have built something meaningful or carried a project across the finish line, but if you don't claim it, someone else will. There's always a fox waiting to swoop in and turn your effort into their applause.

While silence may be a virtue, in the workplace, it's often mistaken for absence. A person who doesn't claim their contribution is like a creature that gives birth and walks away, leaving its creations to be raised and praised by another.

So, own what you've built. Speak for your work before someone else narrates your story. Taking credit isn't arrogance; it's a rightful act of self-respect. It is a declaration that says. *"I was here, and I made this happen."*

In the politics of the workplace, those who stay unseen often end up working for those who don't.

> ***A farmer who tills the soil through every season yet claims no harvest will watch another man walk away with the grain.

Learn How to Present Your Work

Saying *"I love you"* to the wrong person can lead to a lifetime of regret. Similarly, presenting your work to the wrong audience has a similar potential for disaster.

Knowing your audience is not just a courtesy; it is a critical defence.

In the game of professional advancement, you must be aware of the opportunists. They often wear masks of collaboration, offering flattery and false praise while subtly extracting your insights for their own gain.

The moment you let your guard down; revealing too much, too soon, they are poised to exploit the opening. They may co-opt your intellect, using the information you provided as a lever to advance their own agenda.

Be mindful, the cost of trusting the wrong person usually arrives long after the damage is done.

Learn to advocate for yourself

Your workplace is not a home, your boss isn't a guardian, and your colleagues aren't your friends. Everyone in the office has their own agendas and priorities, just like you've got one.

In the realm of professionalism, everyone is like runners in a marathon; fully prepared to compete and win. There are no real enemies, only you and your opponent. Whether you cross the finish line first or they do, there's no help, no shortcuts—just you and the race.

You are one of the runners. Until you reach your finish line, there's no one to carry you forward, only spectators who'll cheer your success or whisper about your fall. So, learn to speak up for your worth, defend your ideas, and claim your space. In this track, silence doesn't grant virtue; it erases the runner who refuses to be seen.

Learn how to be smart

It is said that a well-dressed fool cannot be identified until he speaks, but the moment he does, he reveals himself completely. Being the loudest in the room doesn't make one the smartest; sometimes, knowing when to stay silent carries more weight than speaking ever could.

Only fools learn to speak without listening; the wise first master silence, for it is silence that unveils the truth.

In office politics, this difference is everything. Those who talk too much often expose their cards, while those who stay composed study the game, its players, and hidden alliances. They speak less, but their words carry more weight, not because of volume, but because of timing.

Being smart is not about outspeaking others; it's about outthinking them. It's knowing when to speak, when to hold back, and when silence says more than any argument ever could.

A fool speaks to be noticed; the wise wait to be remembered.

Learn the actual intention of your company

A farmer must understand what kind of soil they are working with and what kind of seeds he is sowing in order to receive a favorable harvest. Similarly, you must discern the intention, motivation, and culture of the place you choose to work and position yourself accordingly.

Jumping into an organization without understanding its culture is like a farmer planting blindly, unaware of the soil's nature or the climate's temperament, risking disappointment instead of growth.

What seems promising at first glance often hides what the soil truly holds. The salary a company offers may appear rewarding, yet it can also be a deceptive lure if its culture conflicts with your personal values or professional aspirations. Many organizations will buy your time but not invest in your growth. They may praise your efforts, promise promotions, or speak of **"family culture,"** yet their true focus often lies in extracting every ounce of your productivity for their benefit.

They may flatter you with empty assurances of *career development* and *work-life balance*, but will discard you once they find no use in you.

Stay alert, stay aware. If growth feels stifled or respect runs thin, walk away before they choose your ending for you.

Learn to understand the matrix of your company

Every workplace has two worlds; the one displayed in charts and titles, and the one that truly governs beneath the surface. The first speaks in designations and reports; the second moves through unspoken alliances and silent exchanges. It is this hidden web—*the matrix*—that decides whose presence carries weight, whose work endures, and whose effort dissolves unnoticed.

Not everyone who leads holds power, and not everyone with power leads. Some move in silent yet alters the course of decisions; their approval shifts tides, their absence reshapes the air in every room. They are the unseen hands steering direction; the *pulse* within the organization.

To read this pulse, you must become observant. Notice who draws attention without demand, whose voice lingers after discussions, whose consent others seek without request. These are the silent gatekeepers of progress.

This is not flattery—it is awareness. Align with those who move the system forward, not those merely suspended within it. Place your effort where it will be recognized, your ideas where they can breathe, and your dignity where it cannot be traded.

Those who fail to sense the matrix often become its prey; those who discern it learn to move through it—*without surrendering their essence to it.*

Learn to continue learning

Whatever title you are holding is rented—not owned. The position you were offered or the job you're currently holding can be easily replaced once your usefulness is no longer visible.

You are like a product displayed in the market, and when marketers find you fresh and useful, they will have you—

give you a title, but when your usefulness wanes, or they find you obsolete, you will be discarded without a second thought. It sounds harsh, yet this world runs on utility, not emotion. You are just one of the products on the shelf vying for continued relevance and utility.

Continue learning to maintain your **"freshness"** and avoid professional obsolescence. Knowledge and skill are the only keys to unlock the future uncertainties. The day you stop learning, you start losing value. What once made you impressive begins to fade into the background, and the applause will eventually stop. The workplace doesn't slow down for those who stop growing, it simply moves past them.

Don't just protect your job—**protect your relevance.** Keep your curiosity alive and your skill sharp. The world rewards only those who stay current and capable, not the title.

Introduction

It was early summer, a bright day that already felt hopeful. I dressed carefully that morning—light brown formal shirt, dark blue nylon pants my elder brother had gifted me for a singing competition, and my white sneakers. After a quick spray of cologne, I looked in the mirror and smiled. For the first time in a while, I felt genuinely confident. I even whispered to myself, *"You look good, bro! Today's your day."*

With my phone, wallet, and bag in hand, I stepped out for the interview. The talent acquisition team had already briefed me about the company's culture and expectations, so I felt prepared.

When I reached the office, the gatekeeper greeted me warmly.
Guard: "Sir, aap ko kahan jana hai?" (Where are you heading, sir?)
Me: "Aaj mera interview hai." (I have an interview today.)
He smiled and said, *"Mere saath aaiye, main madad karta hoon"* (Come with me, I'll help you). He walked me to the reception, where the receptionist already knew my name. She asked me to fill out a form and then guided me to the interview room.

The interview began at 11 am and went on until 3 pm. I met the hiring manager, then the AVP, and finally the

CEO. Surprisingly, the flow felt smooth—like the saying, *"When the morning coffee is good, the rest of the day goes well."*

I walked out satisfied with my performance. That very next day, I received an email and a call from HR with a job offer. I accepted and joined a month later.

The work life

Once I joined the company, the HR manager gave me a brief orientation about its operations, goals, and culture. After that, I was welcomed by the HOD, who explained my roles and responsibilities in detail. To be honest, I was a little overwhelmed and couldn't grasp much. He described all the branches, how the organization was structured, and shared the KPIs for my role. Unlike other companies, each branch had different products, so it was a lot to take in. The HOD understood that it wasn't easy to absorb everything in the first meeting, so he reassured me not to worry and promised to provide brochures and training materials.

Later, I was welcomed by the CEO and then introduced to the team by the HOD. The next day, the team manager gave me a walkthrough of the process and handed me the training materials and brochures.

It took me about a week to understand the process and the products. After that, I was assigned small tasks, and gradually, my responsibilities increased. At the same time, feedback and performance reviews started coming in. My performance feedback was positive, and it didn't take long before I began working closely with my manager. Often, they would ask for my input when dealing with clients and praised my knowledge and presentation skills. They will flatter me and even suggested I should take on more responsibilities to work toward a promotion.

After six months in my department, I was transferred to the operations team, where I managed most of the orders and client data single-handedly. I naively believed that I was performing exceptionally well and would soon be promoted, as I was excelling in my role. As time went on, I was assigned more and more tasks, working harder than anyone else on the team, convinced my efforts would eventually be recognized. During the peak season, I even worked extra hours to ensure the team met deadlines.

But I soon realized I was like the donkey in the old story—the harder I worked, the heavier the load became, and the less I was recognized. After the peak season, the HOD abruptly sent me back to my old department without any explanation. I didn't think much of it at the time, still hoping my hard work would eventually be noticed.

That hope ended during my annual performance review. To my shock, all my efforts had been overlooked. The credit was given instead to my managers and the HOD. To make matters worse, I discovered that a teammate, who hadn't worked nearly as hard, received a higher raise and a better rating from management. Frustrated and confused, I confronted my manager for an explanation, but my concerns were dismissed.

Disheartened, I stopped putting in extra effort and began working only to meet the bare minimum requirements. Predictably, the organization's growth started to decline.

The HOD was summoned by top management to explain the drop in performance and productivity. Instead of addressing the root cause, he tried to save his image by blaming the staff, *including me*, for the downfall. He even went as far as claiming I didn't know how to work, despite my past records.

Eventually, without much discussion or warning, I was suddenly transferred to another company within the group.

Transfer to other company.

Before my transfer, I had an informal conversation with the new manager and the head of department to better understand my roles, responsibilities, liabilities, and the transition to the new company. They readily agreed to all my terms and gave me firm commitments without much hassle. But once I joined, it turned out to be a different story—chaotic and disappointing.

Instead of reporting directly to the manager, they appointed a new team leader and made me report to him. Whenever I tried to discuss any matter with the manager, he would conveniently busy himself with other work to avoid the conversation. To make matters worse, the team leader was passive-aggressive, eager to take credit for the team's work despite having little knowledge of the operations. He micromanaged excessively and criticized the team constantly, leaving no room for productivity.

When I first joined the department, my performance scores were among the top—even better than their existing employees. But after consistently scoring high for several days, the team leader began assigning me random tasks without any pattern or logic. At times, he would act overly friendly and not assign me any tasks at all, leaving me idle the whole day. He even approved continuous leave for me. Naively, I followed his instructions, thinking it was part of maintaining a good working relationship. However, his real motive became clear: to drag down my performance and make management believe I was unfit for the role.

Eventually, I realized I had been transferred as a scapegoat, used to cover up the incompetence of the existing team in front of upper management. Once I understood the toxic games being played, I had no choice but to resign for the sake of both my mental health and my career.

A toxic leader survives only as long as people stay silent. Speak up, set boundaries, and never trade your dignity for a paycheck.

This story may or may not relate directly to me, but it reflects a common reality in many organizations. Power dynamics, hidden agendas, and unfair practices are rampant in corporate setups; especially where managers and self-proclaimed leaders resort to **"toxic leadership"** *to preserve their influence and status. Innocent employees rarely realize the dirty politics at play; they believe their hard work and dedication will be recognized and rewarded, only to have their careers destroyed by the very people they trusted.*

Many young professionals enter organizations with high hopes and ambition, only to be crushed by the harsh realities of toxic leadership, where personal agendas outweigh organizational success. Studies suggest that over 80% of employees experience workplace toxicity in some form, and tragically, some even reach the point of suicide due to depression or related mental health struggles.

Countless talented individuals remain trapped in these environments, slowly losing their self-worth, while manipulative leaders reap the benefits of their labor. With no accountability or justice in place, the cycle continues unchecked. That is why only your wisdom, discernment, and courage can protect you from falling into such traps.

Obtain the power and be rewarded, or ignore it and perish.

Master the art of storytelling.

When trust breaks, even truth looks like a lie, and the mind becomes its own deceiver.

One day, a professor walked into a lecture hall with a jar full of cookies. Before the class began, he distributed them among the students, each receiving a single, warm cookie. Some began eating right away, while others held onto theirs. Once he had finished distributing the cookies, he asked the students, *"How did the cookies taste?"* Some replied, *"Sweet,"* others said, *"Delicious,"* and a few mentioned specific qualities like *"chewy"* or *"crispy."* But none complained.

The professor paused, letting their responses settle. Then he revealed that the cookies were actually made for dogs and never meant for human consumption. Immediately, the class erupted in a mix of disgust and disbelief, with some students even experiencing nausea, trying to rid themselves of the cookies they had just eaten.

A few minutes later, once he had calmed them down, the professor explained that the cookies were, in fact, ordinary human-grade cookies. Still, some students continued to feel **nauseated**, illustrating the powerful influence of preconceived notions on both perception and physical sensation.

He then lectured on the impact of framing effects and cognitive biases, particularly how expectations can override sensory input to shape our entire experience. He asked, *"Would any of you have complained if I hadn't said anything?"* and, *"What if I told you this was a premium cookie made by a star chef, would it change the way you tasted it?"*

After a thoughtful pause, he resumed his lecture: *Everything we perceive and interpret is influenced by the narratives we construct, or the ones handed to us.*

The taste indeed matters, but the story behind it often dictates our ultimate appreciation and experience. Soon, two men entered, carrying an ornate wooden box, no more than two or three feet in size, and placed it gently on the table at the front of the lecture hall. The professor then unveiled an old painting that resembled depictions of the Greek gods and began to weave a tale about its origins.

He claimed it was painted by Botticelli in the 1480s, a period when the artist was at the height of his creative powers, producing masterpieces for the Medici family. He elaborated on the painting's historical significance, its intricate details, and the profound influence it supposedly had on the artistic movements that followed.

The painting, he described, showed the goddess Venus rising from the sea on a giant seashell, her golden hair flowing, her body elongated and almost otherworldly in proportion. On one side, the wind gods Zephyrus and Aura blew her toward the shore; on the other, a maiden stood waiting to cover her with a cloak.

But when the students looked at the painting, it struck them as a cheap imitation. To their eyes, it seemed odd, inauthentic, and far from convincing. Skepticism filled the room; they didn't want to believe him. When the professor asked whether they accepted his claim, a wave of dissenting murmurs and headshakes swept through the lecture hall.

"*Why?*" he asked.

One student responded, *"It might be another trick, and the portrait looks obviously fake, it's too gaudy, and the colors are too bright."*

The professor paused thoughtfully before replying, *"The portrait is, in fact, real."*

He continued, *"It was when I betrayed your trust with the cookies that you became skeptical and began to question everything I said. That is today's lesson. If I had presented the painting first, without the cookie narrative, your perception might have been entirely different. You would likely have accepted its authenticity and perhaps even admired its artistic merit without question. In truth, had I not staged the cookie scene, you would have believed this story, no matter how outlandish."*

He tapped the table with the pen in his hand and told the students, *"When trust is broken, truth itself becomes difficult to believe. We begin to live in skepticism, where even truth struggles to be accepted. Words are sharper than any two-edged sword, they can sever unseen bonds: trust, relationships, reputation, and, most importantly, your future."*

With that, he concluded his lecture.

The Power of Perception

What we see, hear, and taste is never just the thing itself; it is the story we wrap around it. A cookie becomes sweet or sickening, a painting priceless or fake, not solely because of what it is, but because of what we believe it to be. We interpret every experience through the filter of our beliefs, memories, and the narratives that define our world.

Once we understand this, we begin to see that perception is not passive, it is power. The stories we tell can crown a leader or crumble an empire; they can shape a brand, a reputation, or a destiny. Those who master storytelling hold the subtle art of shaping belief, of turning imagination into influence.

This was the essence of what the professor taught in his lecture room. His lesson was not merely about perception but about power; the power to shape belief through story. Long before psychology named it, storytellers understood what only time would later prove that belief is born from imagination.

In ancient Greece, a man named Aesop began life as a slave, poor, voiceless, and insignificant. He owned nothing, not even his freedom. Yet his intellect and command of narrative transformed him into one of history's most enduring storytellers. His fables, rich with moral wisdom, transcended class and time, reaching kings and philosophers who leaned in to listen. Through his words, a slave won his freedom.

The professor's demonstration with the painting was more than an exercise; it was a mirror to the modern world. He showed how easily the mind can be swayed, not by facts, but by the stories wrapped around them. Humanity would rather believe a compelling lie than a dull truth.

Today, the same art moves billions. Advertisements do not sell soap or perfume; they sell beauty, belonging, and desire. Politics, too, thrives not on bare facts but on carefully spun tales of heroes and enemies, fear and hope. Entire nations are stirred more by a single story, repeated with conviction, than by a thousand pages of evidence.

That is the power and the peril of storytelling. Narratives can build bridges or walls, ignite wars or end them, enslave minds or set them free. Once belief takes root, even overwhelming evidence struggles to undo it. The story we accept becomes the truth we live by. And those who understand this do not merely speak; they shape worlds.

Don't Let Loyalty Blind You

Loyalty at work may feel noble, but in a toxic corporate culture, it's like rescuing a snake; you'll be bitten the moment your usefulness ends.

After completing her graduation from Delhi University, Yukti began her career at a BPO in Noida. She was young, diligent, and remarkably resilient. Rotating shifts and heavy workloads never deterred her. When staff shortages arose, she shouldered extra responsibilities. During peak seasons, she even volunteered for weekend shifts. She never questioned orders, never resisted unreasonable tasks, believing that loyalty was the mark of a good employee.

For four years, Yukti served the company with that same conviction. Then life changed; she married and later became pregnant. When her condition made travel difficult, she requested permission to work from home or take leave without pay. The management refused, calling it a policy constraint. A few weeks later, they terminated her employment, due to her physical condition. The same company that once praised her dedication now saw her as a burden.

No one called to ask how she was doing. No message of concern. Just silence. For them, she was a number on a spread sheet, useful when productive, disposable when not.

Yukti's story is not rare. Many employees mistake compliance for loyalty, believing obedience guarantees security. They endure pressure, ignore exploitation, and trust that recognition will come but often, it doesn't.

Organizations in general prioritize profit over employees, choosing office politics over merit and status over humanity. They don't truly care about who you are or what you've done for them in the past; they only care about what you can do for them in the present and the future. Employees are seen as mere resources; they will praise you and keep you as long as you are useful to them, but once your usefulness has expired, they will replace you without hesitation. This is the harsh reality of the corporate world.

In another case. Kartik. For seven years, he led a small marketing team at an education firm, earning a reputation for integrity and performance. His loyalty was unquestioned, until the founder's daughter arrived as the new marketing director. With no experience in the field, she dismissed the team's ideas and replaced strategy with whim. Predictably, results plummeted.

When the losses became visible, blame needed a name. Kartik and his team were scapegoated, dismissed without severance, their years of service reduced to a brief HR email. The real cause, nepotism and incompetence remained untouched.

Such stories echo across countless organizations. When profits fall, loyalty turns invisible, and relationships dissolve into transactions. Hard work, experience, and trust are weighed only against numbers. *They praise you while you serve their interests, but once your utility fades, you vanish from memory.*

Understand the climate of your company.

Be loyal to your growth, not to the illusion of belonging.

Learn the art of chameleon-like adaptation; be loyal to your skills, talents, and career, not to the company. Be loyal when it's worth it, but ready to move on when needed. Offer generous severance rather than clinging to workers whose skills no longer fit your needs. Maintain professional detachment and never let emotional investment cloud your judgment. Your career is your responsibility, and your future depends on how wisely you protect it.

Remember: the office is not your home; your boss is not your father; your colleagues are not your friends. Everyone is there for their own gains and benefits, just as you are. They are not there to care for you, and your boss is not there to protect you. Set clear professional boundaries and be wary of sweet talk and empty praise. You never know when the hissing snake will bite the rescuer or when the loyal sheep will be sent to the slaughterhouse.

It is wiser to shield your sense of self and remain loyal to your own evolution. Be a corporate chameleon. Blend in when required, adapt to change, and shift colors with awareness. Such adaptability is not deceit; it is intelligence. It ensures that no matter how the environment transforms, you will always land on your feet. Those who master adaptability always stay centred even when the world around shifts.

As the *Bhagavad Gita* teaches, attachment, fear, and anger cloud discernment. In the professional realm, attachment to organizations, loyalty to overbearing superiors, or fear of losing favor can become chains that stunt growth. Be wise like the sage. Serve with clarity, not attachment; work with heart, not dependence. The one who clings blindly to loyalty often mistakes bondage for virtue.

Be wise. Offer your best, yet guard your freedom.
Be kind, but not blind.
Be loyal, but never to your own detriment.

The truth is harsh but necessary: companies don't love; they calculate. Your value is weighed in deliverables, not devotion. Once your usefulness fades, even your legacy becomes negotiable. Yukti's loyalty was exploited, and Kartik's integrity scapegoated, both discarded when they ceased to serve convenience. Their dedication deserved respect, yet they were erased by a system that values profit over people.

Maintain your professional distance. Build respect, nurture skill, but never surrender agency. Master the art of chameleon-like adaptation. Learn when to blend, when to stand apart, and when to walk away. That is how one survives and thrives in the modern workplace.

Protect your growth above all else. Your worth is greater than any company's agenda, no matter how sweet the praise or how warm the promises. Loyalty is noble, but blind loyalty is bondage. Be wise enough to serve with heart, yet free enough to walk away with dignity.

> *The Enron scandal of 2001 stands as proof of how devotion can be weaponized. Thousands of employees poured years of hard work, commitment, and even their life savings into a company they trusted. They believed they would be rewarded. Yet, when the company's fraudulent schemes were exposed, the illusion shattered overnight. Jobs vanished and careers were left in ruins. Those who had given everything were discarded without hesitation, their loyalty exploited, their dedication rendered meaningless. Profit, deceit, and self-interest reigned supreme, while workers paid the price for the greed of a few at the top.*
>
> *The Lehman Brothers collapse in 2008 delivered a lesson no less ruthless. Employees who had been loyal, hardworking, and long-standing suddenly found themselves abandoned as the financial giant crumbled*

under mismanagement and reckless risk-taking. Careers disappeared in days, and families lost savings they had entrusted to the system. No amount of loyalty or years of service could shield them from the harsh truth: in a system driven by profit and self-preservation, people are expendable.

The message is brutal and unmistakable: companies don't value devotion, they value usefulness. Loyalty, hard work, and personal sacrifice may earn you temporary recognition, but once your value to the system fades, you are discarded without warning. These cautionary tales remind us that blind loyalty offers no protection. In the corporate world, survival belongs to the adaptable, the discerning, and those who prioritize growth over the illusion of security.

Play Dumb to Obtain Power

Power is the oldest hunger in humankind. Everyone desires power and authority, seeks to control situations and people, and strives to appear smarter and superior, including your boss, seniors, and co-workers. They don't want to be outshone or outperformed. They want to preserve their dominance and feel secure in their status; they will tolerate you as long as they don't feel threatened.

Whatever you do is fine, so long as you don't make them feel inferior or challenge their authority. Project yourself as less capable than you really are. This helps you avoid seeming competitive and lowers the risk of having your ideas dismissed or being seen as a threat.

Allow them to keep their illusion of superiority until the right time. Be patient and bide your time; don't challenge their power or correct them. Instead, carefully and strategically play dumb. Let them believe they're in control and keep them comfortable while you play behind the scenes to your advantage.

Follow their lead, and avoid showing more capability or knowledge than they expect from you. Seek their advice and even make a few strategic mistakes to reinforce the image of your limited ability. Ask them easy questions, and praise them when they offer guidance or correct your mistakes. This builds trust and makes them feel important. But don't overdo it, maintain an airy balance and ensure they don't undermine you. Your game is to lower their guard not to undermine you.

Han Xin was not weak, though he learned early how to appear so. Before he became the mind behind an empire, he walked through markets mocked, endured commands from lesser men, accepted roles that hid his brilliance. Once, a local bully forced him to crawl between his legs. Han Xin did not resist. He understood something most do not learn until it is too late. Power fears exposure more than opposition.

When Liu Bang, later Emperor Gaozu of Han, first encountered him, Han Xin did not announce his genius. He obeyed, listened, waited. He allowed others to feel superior, to believe they led. His patience made him tolerable. His restraint made him useful. In time, when wars demanded minds rather than titles, his true capability surfaced not as challenge, but as necessity.

Han Xin won battles no one else could. He secured kingdoms without demanding the spotlight. Yet history offers a final caution. The moment his brilliance became impossible to ignore, the moment his power stood too clearly on its own, fear replaced trust. The same emperor who relied on him came to see him as a threat. Han Xin was executed, not for failure, but for being seen too fully.

His life leaves a quiet lesson. Power accepts talent only while it feels superior to it. Influence grows best when it moves unseen. Those who survive longest understand when to appear small, when to remain silent, and when to act decisively.

Avoid giving raw Feedback

Nobody likes feedback, even when they ask for it. Never openly criticize your superiors' decisions or actions even if your solution is better. They'll see it as a direct challenge to their authority. Instead, frame your ideas as questions or suggestions, and let them take the credit. This way, you won't appear confrontational or competitive, and they'll be more receptive to your input.

Think of it this way: dealing with authority is like raising a lion as a pet. The lion may enjoy your company, but it never forgets its strength. You must keep it comfortable and never provoke its instinct for dominance or it will turn on you. Feed it well, praise it often, and treat its power with respect. In much the same way, handle your superiors: assure them of their place, keep them secure in their role, and they will grant you room to move. Feed their ego with gentle words and measured humility, and the doors you seek will open with less resistance.

The more you nurture their ego, the more they begin to trust you, and trust is the leash that gives you space to maneuver. Over time, a lion well-fed becomes less quick to bare its teeth. In the same way, authority when flattered, they become docile, lowering its guard and offering you freedom to act. It is then that you can advance with subtle influence, not by force, but by patience.

Yet beware: the higher the ego rises, the dimmer the light of wisdom becomes. An unchecked ego is a gate that bars knowledge from entering the mind. The one who feeds it understands this truth and learns to walk the thin line between praise and manipulation, humility and strategy, until power itself becomes an ally rather than an enemy.

> *The circus trains the vicious lion not by defeating it but by feeding it what it craves **"meat"** and slowly taming it. Similarly, you must learn to appease and flatter your superiors, making them feel important and in control, even as you work behind the scenes to advance your own agenda. The purpose of taming the lion is to make it perform in the circus, just as your goal in flattering your superior is to subtly outwit their power.*

Mirror the cage!

Target the weak spot

Meat is the lion's weakness, the bait that tames its wildness. In the same way, your superiors also have weaknesses you can exploit. Identify their insecurities, fears, egos, and blind spots, and use that knowledge to your advantage. Most people in power crave admiration, respect, emotional validation, and the illusion of superiority. These desires are your levers of influence.

Place each of them at the center of your strategy. Flatter them in the areas where they excel and play to their ego. Praise their leadership, intellect, decision-making, or any quality that reinforces their self-image. This makes them feel important and appreciated, lowering their guard.

Offer just enough to satisfy their ego, but never so much that it arouses suspicion, or they will sense your intentions. Your gestures must appear genuine, even naive; otherwise, you achieve the opposite of what you seek.

Remember, you are not a rival but a tamer; Like a circus trainer guiding a wild beast. Your goal is not to defeat the lion but to make it perform for your benefit. Never provoke or challenge your superiors directly. Instead, keep a posture of humble deference, letting them believe they command the stage while you quietly position yourself to gain ground. This is the essence of "**playing dumb**" to win.

A skilled lion tamer never wrestles the beast; he studies its moods, times his steps, and knows when to advance and when to retreat. Control is not about overpowering but about patience, timing, and restraint. In the same way, learn to read the insecurities of your superiors and move in step with them. Sometimes a pause, a question, or even silence can be more effective than praise, guiding them to lower their guard and grant you the space you seek.

It is not about proving yourself smarter or stronger than them. It is about making them feel more secure and central in their power. Always remember: a lion tamer was never stronger than the lion. He simply understood its weakness and mastered the art of giving it exactly what it craved.

You challenge the lion and you will be eaten; you tame the lion and you will be his master.

Smile to cover the fangs.

Never let them see you angry, frustrated, or upset by their decisions or actions. Maintain a calm, pleasant, and cooperative demeanour, even when you disagree. This makes you appear unthreatening and easy to work with.

Stay humble and follow their lead for now. Show support for their plans and decisions, and avoid offering unsolicited advice, let them feel they are in charge. This softens their attitude toward you. But don't be a doormat; choose your battles carefully and assert yourself only when it serves your strategy.

Keep your true thoughts and feelings hidden, revealing only what they expect to see; a compliant, eager-to-please, deferential subordinate. Disarm them with charm and harmlessness, while the real power simmers beneath the surface. Your role is to appear the hero in their eyes, never the threat.

Understand their deepest desires and insecurities, and blind them with the allure of their own cravings. Make them feel validated, admired, and in control, and they will unwittingly grant you the access and opportunities you seek. Give them satisfaction while quietly taking what you need. Appeal to their self-importance, and you will find all doors open to you. Feed it with a careful blend of deference and calculated praise. The lion tamer's secret is simple: gain the beast's trust by tending to its pride and it will follow wherever you guide it.

Charles Maurice de Talleyrand was not admired for strength, courage, or loyalty. He was feared for his restraint. He served the French monarchy, then the Revolution, then Napoleon, then the restored monarchy again. Each regime destroyed its enemies. Talleyrand outlived them all. This was not luck. It was method.

Napoleon himself noted that Talleyrand never reacted emotionally. When decisions went against him, he did not protest. When dismissed, he did not sulk. When insulted, he appeared unbothered. He agreed publicly, even when he disagreed privately. This made him seem cooperative, useful, safe.

Napoleon trusted men who did not threaten his authority. Talleyrand understood this. He praised Napoleon's intellect, affirmed his leadership, echoed his certainty. He asked questions that allowed Napoleon to arrive at conclusions Talleyrand had already calculated. He never corrected him in front of others. When he advised caution, it was framed as concern for Napoleon's legacy, not opposition to his will.

Privately, historical records show that Talleyrand disagreed with many of Napoleon's campaigns. He believed the emperor was overreaching. Yet he showed no anger, no frustration, no moral outrage. He waited.

While Napoleon believed Talleyrand loyal, Talleyrand quietly maintained relationships with rival powers and preserved his influence within France. When Napoleon finally fell, it was Talleyrand who negotiated with Europe and helped shape the new order. The empire collapsed. Talleyrand retained power.

His strategy was simple and documented. Never appear emotionally reactive. Never challenge authority openly. Let power feel admired and secure. Access follows comfort. Influence follows access.

Build your empire from the shadow

***Power moves best in silence. Those who announce their purpose invite resistance; those who hide it shape destiny.

While your superiors bask in the spotlight of their inflated egos, you should quietly and methodically build your own power base behind the scenes. Accumulate knowledge, skills, connections, and resources that will serve you when the time comes to make your move. Cultivate relationships with influential people both above and below your superiors in the hierarchy. Become their go-to person for information, advice, and problem-solving. Slowly and subtly position yourself as an indispensable asset—someone they cannot afford to lose or upset. All the while, maintain an air of loyalty and deference. In this way, you amass influence without ever threatening your superiors' egos.

Consider John Withson was fired from his position as business development manager after he foolishly had an argument with the head of operation (HOD) over some data discrepancies. Unbeknownst to him, the HOD was a close friend of the CEO, who leveraged that relationship to have John removed. The foolish John was in no way near arguing the authority of the CEO, so he accepted the decision and was ready for the FNF payout. While the dust was settling, John's friends and all the influential people he had supported were waiting and ready to follow John's order. They were ready to give their resignation at any time John called on them.

Soon it came to the attention of all the VP, MD, directors, and the CEO himself. That John was not an expendable cog in the wheel of the company. They realize that removing him will only lead to major organizational disruption. Faced with this dilemma, the company had no other choice than to conduct a management reshuffle and bring back John as a general manager (GM), which was bigger than his initial position. He even demanded the removal of HOD as a condition for his return, which the management agreed to without much hassle.

The power:
Not only can he remove his senior (HOD), but now his influence in the company has grown many folds. All this power he conducted is a direct result of building relationships while playing behind the scenes.

***Removing your superior is not possible for common employees, but it is easy for those who play their cards right.

Louis XIV and Cardinal Mazarin

In 17th century France, a young Louis XIV ascended the throne under the watchful eye of Cardinal Mazarin, the king's chief minister. To the outside world, Louis seemed inexperienced, even pliable—a boy king who relied entirely on his ministers' guidance. Nobles and courtiers, sensing his youth and inexperience, believed they held the reins of power. They flattered him, sought his approval, and maneuvered as if he were easily swayed.

But behind the veil of youth and naivety, Louis was learning. He observed every decision, every alliance, and every subtle shift in loyalty. He allowed the nobles to feed their own egos, to believe they were the architects of France's destiny, while he subtly absorbed knowledge, assessed weaknesses, and built his understanding of statecraft.

He never confronted his courtiers directly. He let them strut, let them believe they were in control, and occasionally appeared to follow their lead. Yet, in every interaction, he positioned himself to gain influence and consolidate authority. Over time, the young king grew from an observer into the master of the court. When the moment was right, he centralized power, reducing the nobles to a controlled presence while he became the undisputed ruler and earned the titled, the Sun King.

Louis XIV's rise was never a display of force. It was the result of patience, careful observation, and the art of letting others feel in control while he learned. Like a skilled lion tamer, he allowed the nobles to strut and parade their influence, never confronting them directly. In doing so, he turned apparent weakness into power, and naivety into mastery. By the time he acted, he did not seize control; he commanded it, effortlessly, because he had shaped the game from the shadows.

Anyone who aspires to mastery must be willing to play the fool, and anyone who seeks success must first make peace with failure.

The promotion playbook

If you never get to taste the fruit of the very plant you've nurtured, then what is the point of doing all the hard work in the first place? Every effort, every sacrifice, deserves its reward; without it, why strive at the very beginning? When you achieve something noteworthy, your dedication should be met with recognition. This is the natural order of things: effort met with reward, ambition met with fulfillment.

The path to promotion is rarely straightforward; it's veiled in secrecy, tangled in unseen forces, and shaped by silent games. Hidden rules and office politics often dictate who rises and who remains unseen, making the process neither fair nor transparent. To claim what's rightfully yours, you must navigate this maze with both precision and grace. It takes more than skill or hard work; it demands an understanding of the unspoken hierarchies, the hidden alliances, and the subtle social currents that run beneath the surface. With this awareness, you can position yourself strategically, ensuring that your efforts are visible, your value recognized, and your place in the hierarchy earned; not by chance, but by choice.

Back in 2023, I had the opportunity to speak with Prakash, a regional manager at an education firm based in Delhi. His insights were profound and invaluable. Originally from Bihar, Prakash completed his Bachelor of Commerce at Delhi University and joined the firm as a business development executive. In this role, he was responsible for connecting with school administrators regarding the exams they conducted and the guidebooks they published. Within just four years—by the age of 25—he had advanced to the position of regional manager, overseeing operations across South India. Securing such a promotion was no small feat, especially for someone from North India, given the language barriers. Despite these hurdles, Prakash's determination and skill allowed him to rise swiftly within the organization.

His playbook was simple. In spite of the communication barriers, he made it a point to connect personally with school administrators and build strong rapport with them. Whenever an issue arose, he addressed and resolved it promptly, earning their trust and respect. As a result, whenever there was an exam or the release of a new guidebook, schools would directly reach out to Prakash for assistance.

From a marketing perspective, this gave him a significant edge, allowing him to secure new contracts and expand his team's reach. Within just two to three years, most schools relied on him for support, making him an indispensable asset to the company. This ultimately solidified his position as regional manager at a remarkably young age.

Unlike his story, if you could recognize my own experience in the organization, you would see that despite my significant contributions and proven track record, I have been overlooked for promotion time and again. I do all the hard work, yet the reward always eludes me—the game is fixed. The HOD and manager take all the credit, reaping the benefits of my efforts while I am left in the cold shadows, burdened beyond measure. Eventually, I walked away from the company, leaving behind my shattered dreams.

Yet, my story is not new. The hallways are lined with the echoes of those who fought the system and lost. Discrimination, nepotism, and a lack of transparency; these are the silent killers that plague the promotion process, stripping deserving individuals of their rightful rewards. Many employees perform their roles faithfully, believing that hard work will be recognized, only to face disappointment and betrayal. But in this game, only those who claw their way to the top succeed—not through merit, but by exploiting the system, wielding connections, and mastering office politics, cutting through the fog while the rest are left behind.

The truth is clear: to get what you deserve, you must learn the art of office politics. Prakash earned his promotion by building relationships, gaining trust, and proving his value to customers, all while keeping his ear to the ground for opportunities. The trust and network he built became his greatest source of power, so much so that removing him from the company would have been a gift to the competitors. That influence ultimately became the key to cracking the code of promotion.

> *It is not the will of the company or the favoritism of the boss that determines your fate, but your ability to play the game with finesse and cunning. The hidden rules of the system are not designed to reward the most skilled or hardworking, but those who can navigate the murky waters of office politics both strategically and tactfully.*

In the promotion playbook, I use **NURSE** as an acronym to summarize the key strategies:

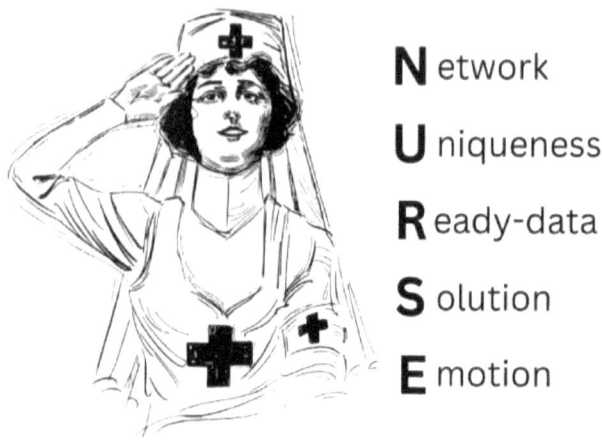

N etwork

U niqueness

R eady-data

S olution

E motion

Network, Uniqueness, Ready data, Solution to the problems, and Emotions

Let's unpack each of these in more detail:

Network: Building a network is like constructing a human body, where connections act as the veins and arteries that keep the system functioning. Our brain serves as the central commander—it holds the knowledge, skills, and vision. Yet, on its own, it is powerless without the support of other body parts. It cannot execute tasks without the hands, legs, eyes, and so on. Similarly, your skills, knowledge, and hard work will not be sufficient if you lack the right connections and networks within your organization.

You must forge alliances, cultivate relationships, and build a web of support that can vouch for your capabilities and champion your cause when the time comes for promotions. This includes your superiors, peers, and even subordinates—anyone who can attest to your value and influence decision-makers. Let your network be your secret weapon, wielded strategically to tip the scales in your favour. When the time comes, let your network act as your hands, legs, and eyes, serving as your conduit to your desire.

Uniqueness: It is much easier to recognize a single green apple in a basket of red ones. To stand out from the crowd, you must identify and hone your unique qualities, your skills, knowledge, and expertise that set you apart from your peers. Ask yourself: What makes you indispensable to the organization? What value can you provide? What problems can you solve that others cannot? Uncover these traits and refine them until they shine. Let them become your card in the game of promotions, a ticket that carries you upward.

Make your contributions and the value you bring to the company visible to those who have the power to uplift you. Be strategic and ensure that decision-makers recognize your unique contributions, skills, and leadership potential as qualities that make you the ideal candidate for the role. Like a chameleon, adapt strategically and let them see the parts of you that fit their needs.

Ready Data: In the game of promotions, data is your ammo. Arm yourself with a well-organized arsenal of evidence, metrics, and accomplishments that demonstrate your capabilities and the impact you've had on the organization. Prepare a dossier of your achievements and quantifiable results to build a strong case for your promotion. When the opportunity arises to advocate for yourself, strike with this ready-made ammunition, leaving no room for doubt or question your viability.

Remember, decision-makers are looking for tangible proof, not just empty claims. Equip yourself with hard data and measurable metrics, not just stories of your contributions. While stories are a great way to highlight your impact, they must be supported by numbers that back them up. Together, they are like a gun and ammunition; stories are the gun, and data is the ammunition that makes it lethal. Without proven data, your story is like a gun without bullets. Hence, you must always be ready with the data to validate your case.

Solution to the problem: Organizations are constantly seeking individuals who can solve problems and enhance efficiency. To gain an edge in the promotion race, position yourself as the go-to person for solutions. Start by identifying the pain points and challenges within your department or the organization—particularly those that your boss or decision-makers are struggling with. Then, master the art of anticipation by crafting innovative approaches and addressing these issues in a way that highlights your value and leadership potential.

Be the hero who steps in with timely, impactful resolutions, easing the burdens of your boss or decision-makers. By doing so, you'll position yourself for the rewards and recognition you desire but also establish yourself as an indispensable leader who drives meaningful change.

Emotion: The path to the top is not just about facts and figures; it's also about stirring emotions. After all, decision-makers are human; they feel and react just like everyone else, and those feelings can profoundly shape their judgment. Build genuine connections with your boss and other decision-makers by fostering trust, loyalty, and empathy. When they feel understood and emotionally invested in your success, they will be more inclined to champion your cause and put their weight behind your promotion.

Cultivate a positive rapport, demonstrate your commitment to the company's mission, and show that you're not just in it for yourself—but for the greater good of the organization. Weave your stories with an emotional thread that resonates with decision-makers, leaving them inspired and building confidence in your ability to lead. In doing so, you'll effortlessly command the power to enchant their minds and hearts, drawing them irresistibly to your cause.

Master these arts of **NURSE**, and you'll not only rise above the rest but effortlessly claim the promotion that's been waiting for you all along. Your **network, uniqueness, ready data, solutions, and emotions**—these are the keys that will unlock the doors to your career advancement. With these keys in hand, you won't just rise; you'll command the room, leaving success no choice but to follow. This is your moment to shine, not just succeed.

Let them take the credit while you take the crown.

The need to be seen as the smartest person in the room is the quickest way to remain a pawn.

Power in the workplace is rarely about who works the hardest; it's about who understands the game best. Recognition may be the visible prize, but influence—the kind that bends outcomes and shapes decisions is the true currency of power. While others chase applause, learn to build advantage through insight and timing. Let them have the spotlight; *you*, after all, are designing the stage itself.

True mastery in the game of promotion is not about wrestling for credit but directing perception. Those who crave validation are often easy to guide, for they reveal what they need most; praise, attention, and reassurance. Give them that, and they will give you everything else. The art lies in restraint: staying composed while others compete for visibility, keeping your ambition cloaked behind grace.

History offers a timeless example in **Zhuge Liang**, the famed strategist of China's Three Kingdoms era. Though he was the mind behind every major victory of the Shu kingdom, he never sought the glory for himself. He let his ruler, Liu Bei, stand as the face of success, while he quietly shaped every outcome from behind the curtain. To him, endurance mattered more than recognition, and restraint proved stronger than display. By allowing others to shine, he became irreplaceable—the unseen force that sustained an entire empire.

In any hierarchy, those who master perception rule the unseen realm. The wise do not demand acknowledgment; they position themselves where acknowledgment becomes inevitable. So let them take the credit, because when the dust settles, it's not the applause that matters, but the authority. You don't need the crowd to see your crown. You only need to wear it well.

Let your influence grow so immense that recognition becomes inevitable, they will have no choice but to acknowledge your worth.

Focus on your one true desire

A powerful and majestic lion does not rely on roaring loudly or baring its sharp teeth to attract prey, nor does it chase after every passing gazelle. Instead, it concentrates its energy on a specific target, patiently waiting for the right moment to strike with precision and force. In the same way, you must hone your focus and direct your energy toward the goal you truly desire, rather than scattering your efforts across countless distractions.

Identify your genuine ambition, align your actions with purpose, and pursue it with laser-like precision, just as a lion zeroes in on its prey.

Cesare Borgia, an Italian nobleman, politician, and condottiero (mercenary leader) during the Renaissance, was known for his cunning and strategic alliances. With sharp focus on his goals, he formed numerous political and military partnerships to expand his power in Italy, ultimately becoming one of the most influential figures of his time. However, his constant shifting of loyalties and alliances made him appear duplicitous to many, which contributed to his downfall. After his father's death, Cesare lost his primary source of support, and former allies turned against him. His opportunistic alliances ultimately led to his demise; he was imprisoned and later killed in 1507. The lesson here is not to emulate Cesare Borgia's unethical pursuit of power, but to learn from the dangers of spreading oneself too thin and forming too many alliances.

When chasing your true desires, it is essential to adopt the lion's fierce focus and decisiveness while avoiding the pitfalls of excessive or indiscriminate alliance-building, a mistake that ultimately plagued Cesare Borgia. Hone yourself with a clear vision, and let that singular purpose guide your actions. Fix your gaze on what you crave and pursue it with a hunger that refuses to be denied. In this way, you meet the craving that only your true prize can fulfil.

Build your reputation to obtain recognition.

Your legacy is not defined by what you accomplish alone, but by how the world sees and remembers your actions. Talent and effort matter, but lasting influence is built on integrity, service, and the trust you inspire in others.

One of the greatest architects in history died alone ignored and mistaken for a beggar. Antoni Gaudí, the visionary behind the Sagrada Família, left behind a legacy of breathtaking design, yet in his final moments, the very city he reshaped failed to recognize him.

A leading figure of the Modernism movement, Gaudí was celebrated for his imaginative architectural style that fused Gothic, Art Nouveau, and organic forms. His most famous creation, the Sagrada Família, remains an enduring testament to his genius. Other remarkable works include Park Güell, Casa Batlló, and Casa Milà (La Pedrera).

Tragedy struck on June 7, 1926, during one of Gaudí's daily walks to the Sant Felip Neri church, where he often went to pray and confess. A tram hit him, leaving him gravely injured. Dressed in his customary modest clothing, he was mistaken for a beggar and left unattended for hours. It wasn't until the following day that Mosén Gil Parés, the chaplain of the Sagrada Família, recognized him. By then, his condition had deteriorated beyond recovery. Gaudí succumbed to his injuries on June 10, 1926.

Despite dedicating his life to shaping Barcelona's skyline, Gaudí became invisible in his moment of greatest need. The same city that marveled at his masterpieces failed to recognize the man behind them; all because he disregarded fame and status, choosing instead to live for his art and faith, with no outward sign of his brilliance or influence.

While mastering one's desires is vital, a good reputation can open doors that talent alone cannot. When your contributions go unnoticed, much of the purpose behind your work fades. Humility is admirable, but visibility matters. Recognition ensures your efforts have impact. Gaudí's tragic end was not the result of his devotion, but rather the consequence of his extreme modesty and lack of self-advocacy.

In my own experience, I learned a similar lesson the hard way. During my time at a company, I worked tirelessly, exceeding expectations, taking on extra responsibilities, and supporting other departments, hoping that my dedication would be recognized and rewarded. Instead, my manager perceived me as a threat. They began to quietly undermine me, assigning impossible tasks, taking credit for my work before the directors, and turning my achievements into their own. (Introduction)

For nearly two years, I endured this without acknowledgment or promotion, until the situation became unbearable and I was forced to resign. By the time I realized what had happened, it was too late to repair my reputation. I knew my value within the department, yet I had failed to make it visible. I worked harder than anyone else, but no one saw it. In the end, all my effort became the wind beneath my manager's wings.

"Silence may carry wisdom, but recognition gives it voice."

The Politics of Recognition

Rungsung Suisa; a Naga politician from northeast India—stands as a remarkable example. His approach to politics required no campaigning, self-promotion, or lofty promises to voters. Instead of chasing attention, he spent his time in quiet reflection and simple activities that brought him peace, yet he won the election with a landslide victory.

He rose to prominence not through grand speeches or performative acts, but through genuine concern for his people and visionary leadership. Unlike most politicians, he avoided the corrupt tactics of vote-buying, smear campaigns, and empty promises. He chose instead to understand people's struggles and focus on solving them, which made him one of the most respected and trusted figures in the region. Beyond politics, Suisa was also known as a teacher, missionary, revolutionary, and thinker —a man of rare integrity and depth.

In a similar spirit, the late Thomas Sankara, a revolutionary leader from Burkina Faso and one of Africa's most distinctive political figures of the 20th century, was renowned for his honesty, courage, and unwavering commitment to the people. He never hesitated to speak truth to power, openly criticizing the corrupt elite and standing firm in defense of ordinary citizens.

On a global scale, Mahatma Gandhi, one of the most iconic leaders of the 20th century, placed greater emphasis on spiritual growth and moral leadership than on political maneuvering or self-promotion. His principles of nonviolence and civil disobedience inspired millions, ultimately leading to India's independence and securing his legacy as the Father of the Nation.

Together, these examples show that while personal achievement and contribution are vital, it is equally important to cultivate a positive public image and ensure that your efforts are visible. A strong reputation amplifies your influence; it opens new doors, attracts opportunities, and preserves your legacy.

Suisa was celebrated for his integrity and dedication, Siddique for his fearlessness and honesty, and Gandhi for his moral leadership. Each reminds us that reputation is not vanity—it is validation. It helps people recognize who you are, what you stand for, and why your work matters. When your name carries trust, your actions gain meaning, and your rewards naturally follow.

> *Truth loses its power when the world cannot see the one who carries it.*

Author's Favourite

One of the most admired figures in modern history is Nelson Mandela, the iconic leader of South Africa's anti-apartheid movement. Imprisoned for 27 years for his fight against racial oppression, Mandela never wavered in his principles or his vision of a just and equal society. His dignity, resilience, and unbreakable moral compass inspired millions around the world.

Through his leadership and moral authority, Mandela helped negotiate the peaceful end of apartheid and laid the foundation for a multiracial democracy. In 1994, South Africa held its first democratic elections, and Mandela became the nation's first Black president.

As president, he chose reconciliation over revenge. To heal a wounded nation, he established the Truth and Reconciliation Commission, addressing the crimes of apartheid through forgiveness and accountability. His leadership was defined by humility, compassion, and unity, earning him respect from both allies and former adversaries. Mandela's reputation was not built through self-promotion, but through integrity, moral courage, and selfless service.

The reputation and influence of Nelson Mandela stand as a powerful counterpoint to the self-serving models of modern politics. Through his unwavering belief in equality, Ubuntu, and forgiveness, he wielded his moral authority to achieve historic transformation—far beyond what mere political maneuvering or personal ambition could ever accomplish.

His life remains a timeless reminder of the transformative power of a reputation grounded in service to others, a legacy that continues to inspire generations to lead with heart, humility, and honor.

> *Reputation is the bridge between what you do and how the world remembers you. Without it, even the most sincere efforts risk being buried in obscurity.*

The Nature of Reputation

While the importance of reputation is well understood in human societies, it holds equal weight in the natural world, where it often determines survival and success. In many species, reputation acts as a silent yet powerful force—shaping hierarchies, guiding behaviour, and ensuring the cohesion of the group.

In elephant herds, for instance, the matriarch's reputation is vital to the safety and survival of the entire family. An experienced and respected matriarch can lead her herd to hidden water sources, fertile grazing grounds, and safe pathways—decisions that often mean the difference between life and death. Similarly, within a pride of lions, the alpha male's reputation sustains his dominance, deters challengers, and secures access to mates and territory. Wolf packs and chimpanzee troops, too, display intricate social systems in which an individual's standing within the group depends on the reputation it earns through behavior and consistency.

On an individual level, animals build and maintain reputation through repeated displays of desirable traits such as strength, intelligence, care, or resourcefulness. A male gorilla that consistently defends his family, shares food, and shows restraint in conflict earns respect as a reliable and protective leader. In contrast, within a school of fish, a swift and elusive swimmer may gain a reputation as a skilled escape artist, its agility helping it evade predators and survive longer than others.

Reputation allows animals to establish trust, respect, and cooperation, fostering harmony within their groups. It shapes how others respond to them, just as it does among humans. Across species, reputation functions as a universal currency of trust, reducing conflict, strengthening alliances, and increasing the chances of both individual and collective success.

The Universal Power of Reputation

The parallels between human and animal societies reveal the universal importance of reputation in navigating social dynamics and achieving success. Whether human or animal, a strong reputation built on integrity, leadership, and service to others can be a transformative force, fostering trust, cooperation, and social cohesion. Just as Nelson Mandela leveraged his moral authority to dismantle apartheid, a respected matriarch in an elephant herd can ensure the survival and well-being of her family. Reputation allows individuals to earn the respect of their communities, reduce conflict, and create opportunities for remarkable achievements.

When seeking influence, status, or leadership, building a reputation aligned with your values and goals is essential. This requires demonstrating competence, character, and commitment in a way that earns trust and admiration. A soldier gains respect by showing courage and concern for their unit; a politician commands confidence through integrity, vision, and dedication to the public good; a corporate leader inspires others through competence, honesty, and the ability to guide effectively.

Still, every reputation carries its own risk; it can open the door of fragility. The very actions that build trust can, if misaligned or misjudged, quickly erode it. Missteps, recklessness, or unethical behavior can undo years of effort almost overnight. Just as a teacher cannot wield force to gain respect, and a warrior cannot rely on sentiment alone in battle, one must carefully align actions with desired perception. Mastering this balance is akin to learning the art of the chameleon—adapting to circumstances while remaining true to core principles.

Ultimately, reputation is both currency and legacy. It is fragile, yet powerful; silent, yet visible. Whether in human society or the animal kingdom, it magnifies influence, unlocks opportunities, and amplifies the impact of one's actions. By cultivating a reputation rooted in integrity, service, and consistent excellence, you ensure that your contributions are recognized and that your legacy endures long after your immediate efforts are complete.

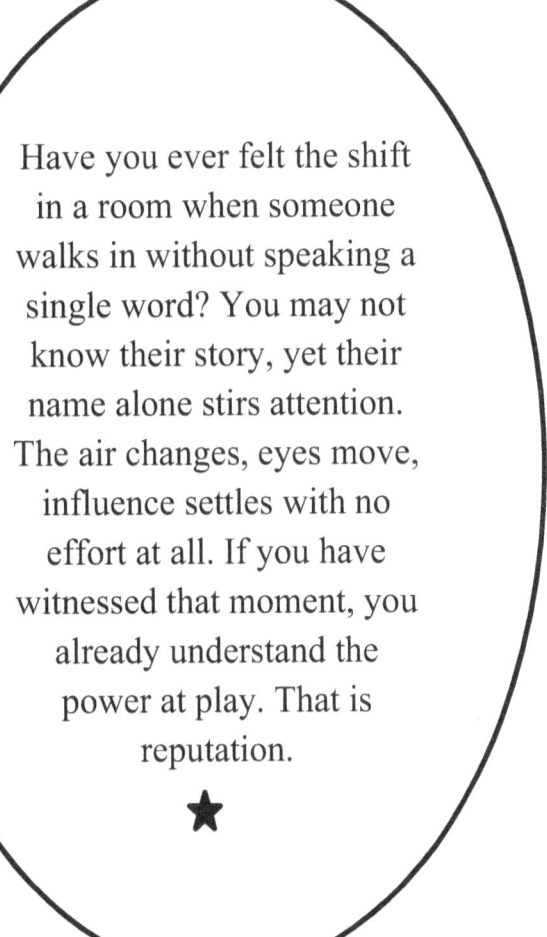

Have you ever felt the shift in a room when someone walks in without speaking a single word? You may not know their story, yet their name alone stirs attention. The air changes, eyes move, influence settles with no effort at all. If you have witnessed that moment, you already understand the power at play. That is reputation.

★

Build Your Brand to Obtain Authority.

What you do builds your skill, but what you reveal builds your career. People are drawn to the story they understand, not the struggle they missed.

In the high-fashion world, where exclusivity is the currency of prestige, luxury brands guard their image with an iron grip. For names like Louis Vuitton, Burberry, and Chanel, a simple markdown isn't just a price cut—it's a threat to their legacy. To preserve their products as emblems of wealth and status, these brands have often resorted to extreme measures. Take Burberry, for instance: in 2018, the fashion house made headlines when it was revealed that it had burned £28.6 million ($36 million) worth of unsold merchandise in a single year. The reason? To prevent those pristine coats, handbags, and accessories from ending up in discount bins or counterfeit markets. After all, in the luxury world, scarcity breeds desire, and excess—if not carefully managed—can unravel a brand's exclusivity.

Luxury brands don't just police their products; they also carefully curate their consumer base. Imagine, for example, a luxury label that donates its entire unsold inventory to charity at the end of each season. What would happen? While this may appear to be a noble gesture, it would dilute the brand's prestige and cachet. Consumers would no longer perceive the brand as exclusive or aspirational. Put simply, a queen would hardly covet a dress worn by a commoner, just as a wealthy man would never wish to wear the same suit as his butler. Or consider this: if gold were as common as stone, would it still be considered a precious metal?

Likewise, your personal brand matters in your professional life. Just as luxury houses protect their image, you must carefully cultivate your own professional identity. How do you want people to perceive you? What kind of authority do you want to project? These choices speak volumes when it comes to building your reputation.

You attract opportunities based on how you present yourself, and you are judged by how others perceive you. Nobody cares who you are behind closed doors; what matters is what the world sees. Like the luxury brands, you must be intentional about your image and deliberately control what others see of you.

Never lower your standards or compromise your principles in pursuit of temptation. *"Donation"* may sound noble, but for luxury brands, it can be a betrayal of their very essence. To maintain your authority and distinction, you must sometimes let opportunities slip away, just as luxury houses destroy unsold goods to protect their image.

What is lost by discarding one rotten potato if it saves the entire harvest from ruin?

When you are seeking promotion or visibility within your organization, learn to be selective. Let go of people or associations that do not align with your identity; otherwise, they will only dilute your career. Be like the luxury brands; release what diminishes you, and focus instead on crafting the image that commands respect and authority.

Your Brand is Your Bait

Elon Musk doesn't just sell electric cars or build rockets; he sells a vision of the future. His personal brand is defined by bold ambition and a fearless approach to risk. Through Tesla, SpaceX, and X, he has cultivated the image of a visionary innovator (*a real-life Tony Stark, if you will*.) Bill Gates doesn't just sell software; he sells philanthropy and global development. Dwayne Johnson "The Rock" doesn't just act in movies; he sells an image of strength, motivation, and charismatic leadership. Every successful individual in the public eye has carefully cultivated their personal brand. Admiration, luxury lifestyle, wealth, power, and influence—these are the currencies that many seek to acquire.

How do you want people to recognize you? What skills or qualities do you want to be known for? These are crucial questions when pursuing authority and success in your career. You must deliberately shape your image to reflect how you want to be perceived and what your audience values most. Just as luxury brands fiercely guard their image, you must also be selective in how you present yourself.

Choose your bait wisely to catch the fish you want.

Ever wondered why so many celebrities reveal their bodies in the media? Or why they dress in certain ways? It's not accidental. It's less about attraction and more about commanding attention, often to advance hidden agendas; whether for money, fame, or influence. There is always intent behind their choices. It is much like a fisherman casting bait to lure fish. Celebrities use their bodies and images as bait to attract media attention and public curiosity, all to achieve commercial or social goals. But beyond appearance, you too must be intentional about the way you communicate, the associations you build, and the experiences you create. Your personal brand is your bait: it determines the audience you draw and the opportunities you secure.

A fisherman who puts a worm on the hook may catch small fish, but the one who uses fish as bait catches something bigger. Likewise, a celebrity who relies only on body exposure may capture the attention of the shallow-minded, but a professional who highlights skills and expertise will attract the attention of decision-makers and influencers. It is always about the bait you choose and the kind of *"fish"* you want to catch.

Be clear about your intentions and strategy. Think carefully about the kind of recognition you want to earn. If you are aiming for promotion within your company, brand yourself in front of your boss as a reliable, trustworthy, and irreplaceable employee. Understand what your boss values; since they hold the power to promote you and shape your image accordingly.

Consider Arvin Kumar, who joined his company as a fresher. Within a year, he was promoted to manager, and within three years, he became the youngest director in his company's history. His rise was not by chance. Beyond his skills and deep understanding of operations, he mastered organizational politics and strategically shaped his personal brand to align with the expectations of the decision-makers. By consistently projecting loyalty, diligence, and trustworthiness, he stood out and he was rewarded.

My own story, however, was quite different. As I mentioned in an earlier chapter, I not only lost my job but also had to endure the dirty politics played by senior colleagues. Despite my hard work and contributions, I was overlooked by decision-makers and betrayed by both my manager and HOD, all because I failed to manage my personal brand. *I became the donkey in the proverb; always chasing the carrot I carried, expecting to reach it, only to be met with the stick instead.*

Office politics and personal branding

Hard work, loyalty, or experience alone will not guarantee the promotion or visibility you deserve. In fact, they can sometimes backfire, breeding enmity and mistrust among colleagues who see you as a threat to their fiefdoms and influence. If your performance outshines your manager's, rather than supporting you, they may feel threatened and find ways to undermine or sideline you. They will see you as a challenge to their authority and will look for any opportunity to eliminate you. *(Always remember how I was played by my seniors.)*

Aruna Kuang is a perfect example of someone who mastered the art of personal branding. She joined an investment banking firm as a telemarketer, and within a year, she overtook the manager's position in her department. Her strategy was simple; she played the **dumb** employee in front of her manager, while presenting herself as a hardworking, loyal, and reliable employee to the decision-makers. *Cunning, right?*

Aruna's strategy may sound ruthless, but strategies like this have existed long before the corporate world. The ancient Naga warriors never allowed their footprints to be tracked by their enemies. During battle also known as hunting season, they would follow the enemy's trail, defeat them, and take their heads as trophies. To avoid being tracked themselves, they removed their sandals, reversed them, and wore them backward so their footprints pointed in the opposite direction, confusing the enemy.

Aruna did the same. She wore the sandals of a **dumb** employee, but her real footprints led straight to the manager's chair. By confusing her manager, she avoided being seen as a threat, while at the same time impressing decision-makers with her consistent hard work, loyalty, and trustworthiness. This is the art of personal branding.

> *Have you ever wondered why some of your colleagues—half as capable as you, receive double the rewards? On top of that, they get the lion's share of the credit, while you're left following their unprofessional orders. Meanwhile, the seniors turn a blind eye, even when they know there's foul play at work or do they really?*
>
> *There could be several reasons for this: favoritism, lack of transparency, or office politics. But the solution lies in your personal branding. The purpose of branding is to shape how your target audience (your seniors) perceives*

you, so you can achieve your desired goals, whether that's a promotion, a raise, or simply greater visibility within the organization.

Remember the fisherman who uses small fish as bait to catch bigger fish? What kind of bait are you putting on your hook to attract your boss and other decision-makers? Once you understand the bait, you'll find your path to promotion.

Learn the art of argument.

In the Game of Influence, Staying Silent Can Stall Your Career—Learn When to Speak, Whom to Persuade, and How to Master the Politics to Advance Your Position.

A mere pawn, small and often overlooked, has the power to end the game if placed with precision and supported by the right force. Likewise, in the battlefield of words, victory belongs to those who position themselves wisely, armed with the right strategies and techniques

Aristotle, the great philosopher, identified the fundamentals of rhetorical invention—the art of crafting a compelling argument. In his view, a rhetorician must observe *"in any given case, all available means of persuasion."* This principle of rhetorical invention has endured through the centuries, shaping the way we communicate and influence others. In the art of argument, you are not merely reciting facts but carefully selecting and arranging them to sway your audience. The goal is not just to inform but to persuade, to shape meaning, and ultimately to fulfil your intent. **This philosophical groundwork became the basis for later rhetoricians, most notably Cicero, who transformed theory into structured practice.**

They trained students to argue for specific propositions; whether of fact, value, or policy, that had been judged the most fitting and compelling. This strategic approach to invention stands in contrast to the more open-ended *"say anything just to say something"* mentality, which weakens an argument. With a clear proposition in mind, you can concentrate your efforts on finding the most effective means of support. Your task is to recognize the strongest appeals and wield them with precision, for persuasion is won not by force, but by mastery of placement.

Presenting Your Argument to the Right People

In rhetoric, a strong argument alone is never the full story. You also need to read the room, sense the mindset of your listeners, and shape your message in a way that reaches them. Many people speak with conviction yet gain nothing, not due to lack of merit, but due to missing the ears that matter. Countless professionals present brilliant ideas to the wrong crowd, or speak at the wrong moment, then wonder why nothing changes. The wiser move is to understand who holds the key, when their attention opens, and how your message can meet their expectations. Influence grows when your voice lands in the right place at the right time.

Within many workplaces, authority often moves in a single direction. Managers, HOD, and HR, each of them upholds a shared structure that keeps their influence intact. Supporting a challenge from below would shake the very system that protects their role. Their unity is not built on loyalty or friendship; it is built on strategy. They operate like seasoned players in a power game, choosing moves that secure control. When they stand together, the structure becomes almost impossible to breach, keeping every decision tilted toward their interests. Such dynamics shift from place to place, yet the pattern often remains the same, revealing how tightly power holds its ground.

Picture this: you walk into a room where three chairs are already occupied. You are the fourth person, left standing, with no extra seat in sight. The rule is simple: if you want to sit, someone must leave. But here lies the challenge—no one gives up a seat willingly unless they see an advantage in doing so.

You now face two choices. First, you could use your wit to persuade one of them to stand, convincing them that yielding the seat serves their interest or protects their reputation. Second, you could bypass persuasion altogether and appeal to the true owner of the chairs—the authority behind the arrangement—presenting a case so compelling that they grant you the right to sit.

This isn't about chairs; it's about power, influence, and strategy. In an organization, the principle is the same. The manager, the head of department and HR are like those three seated figures. They secured their positions through alignment and mutual understanding, and they will not allow anyone to disrupt that balance. They don't see you as someone to assist; they see you as a potential threat to their carefully constructed authority.

You cannot simply expect a place at the table; you must grasp the politics, the dynamics, and the mindset of those already seated. They are not merely occupying their positions—they are defending them. And unless you can outmaneuver their alliance, you will remain standing, waiting for a seat that may never be offered.

So the question remains: **how will you claim your seat?**

> *The moment you set your sights on a promotion, the person in the seat becomes your rival—your advancement depends on taking their position. Pursuing a managerial role inherently implies the displacement of the current manager. Recall the three chairs: if you want to sit, someone must rise. Do you genuinely believe someone comfortably settled in their seat will step aside willingly for you?*

If you want to be the king on the chess board, you must remove the existing king. If you want to sit on the chair, someone has to give up their seat. If you want to be the manager, then the current manager has to be displaced. The game is brutal but this is the only way.

The unwritten law of office politics

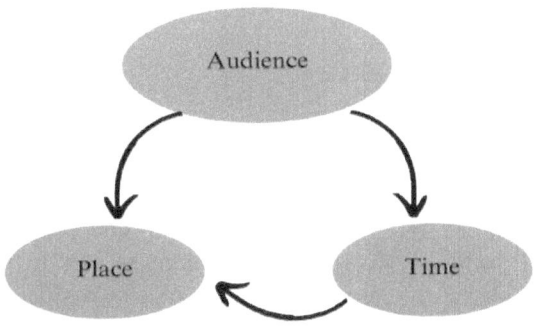

There are three circles you must understand which I called ATP (Audience, Time, and Place.)

Audience: Every argument has a purpose; it's not just about sharing information but about fulfilling a deeper need. That's why the first step is to identify who truly holds the power to decide. Who are they? What drives them? And perhaps most importantly, what do they fear? Understanding their motives, interests, and biases is the key to unlocking their attention. Only then can you craft an argument that resonates with them on a deeper level. Speak to their hearts, align with their thoughts, and your argument will not just be heard—it will be felt.

In my introduction I wanted a promotion; I fought for it, argued for it, but I was speaking to the wrong person. My direct manager never had the power to make that decision. The real decision-makers were the directors. Had I understood their priorities, their concerns, and what truly motivated them, my approach would have been different. Instead of wasting time trying to convince my manager, I should have directed my efforts toward those who actually held the authority. No matter how strong the argument may be, if it's made to the wrong audience, it leads nowhere.

Time: Equally important as knowing your audience is understanding the right time to present your argument. Even the most brilliant message will fall flat if delivered at the wrong time. A powerful argument is not just about logic; it's about mastering the art of timing. Think of it this way; who eats bread after dinner? Who plans a wedding on the day of a funeral? Timing shapes perception, which in turn shapes influence. To make an impact, you must know when to speak and when to wait.

We eat food to satisfy our hunger, not to scald our tongues on hot soup. Likewise, your argument should fulfill its purpose, not overwhelm or exhaust your listener. If you present your argument at the wrong time, it will feel like serving hot soup—unpleasant and hard to digest. Carefully consider the context, the mood, and the current events that might impact how your words are received.

Place: The final piece of the puzzle is where you present your argument. Just as you wouldn't deliver a speech in the middle of a busy street, the setting of your argument matters; when you control the setting, you control the narrative. The physical space, ambiance, and context all influence how your message is received. You wouldn't confront a director about your manager's misbehavior in front of that manager or the entire staff. Instead, a wise approach would be to arrange a private meeting with the director, where you can present your case calmly and professionally. This way your argument is not overshadowed by the wrong environment.

> ***Note:-*** *Understand the nature of your organization, its power dynamics, decision-making processes, and the true center of influence. Study each player's motivations, fears, and biases. This is how you'll identify whom to target, when to strike, and how to frame your message for maximum impact. Precision, patience, and timing are everything; a well-crafted argument delivered at the right moment can move mountains, while the same argument presented carelessly falls on deaf ears. Success does not favour those who speak first or loudest; it favours those who understand the room and strike with clarity and authority. Your argument is your weapon; wield it wisely, and the seat you desire will not remain out of reach.*

Framing your message for clarity

Clarity is the spine of every effective argument. You may speak with passion, carry strong evidence, or stand firm in your conviction, yet if your message feels scattered, your listener will drift before your point even lands. A clear message does not happen by accident; it is built with intention. It begins with stripping your thoughts down to their essence, uncovering the single idea you want your audience to walk away with.

Think of your message as a beam of light. The more focused it is, the farther it travels. When your thoughts wander, your message weakens. When your words overflow, your listener retreats. Clarity demands discipline. It asks you to choose what truly matters, simplify what feels tangled, and remove anything that dilutes your core point.

> *Confusion loses the listener, but clarity commands the room. Tighten your thoughts to widen your impact.*

A strong argument flows smoothly when each idea connects without confusion. Your listener should feel guided, not lost. They should sense direction from your very first sentence. This is why clarity also requires structure. Begin with the heart of your message, support it with clean reasoning, and close in a way that leaves no room for misunderstanding. Clarity is not just about what you say; it is also about what you avoid. You shield your message from unnecessary details or emotional clutter that weakens your impact. When your message is crystal clear, even a few well-chosen words can leave a stronger mark than a long, wandering explanation.

Using Emotion with Intention

Emotion carries a force that logic alone can never reach. In any argument, especially within office politics, emotion becomes the subtle force that shifts people before they even notice it happening. Facts inform the mind, yet emotion conquered; it shapes perception, softens resistance, and opens doors that reason cannot unlock on its own.

When emotion is used with intention, it turns your message into an experience. *A calm tone can project confidence in a way no statistic can. A gentle pause can draw a room closer. A sincere expression can shift the energy of a conversation.* Even a touch of warmth can ease tension and invite cooperation. Emotion helps your listener feel your message rather than simply hear it.

This is the subtle art of influence. People pay attention to how you speak, how you hold yourself, and how your presence makes them feel. Emotion becomes a signal of sincerity, a sign that your words carry meaning beyond the surface. *It gives your argument depth. It gives your message color. It gives your voice weight.*

To use emotion with intention is to communicate in more than words. It is choosing the right tone to guide understanding, the right expression to build trust, and the right energy to draw others toward your point. Logic shapes the structure of your argument, yet emotion breathes life into it.

When both move together with clarity, your message travels farther. It stays with people longer. It becomes something they remember. In the art of argument, emotion is not just a tool; it is the invisible thread that ties your message to the hearts of those who listen.

Argument for Solution

Every argument reaches its true purpose only when it leads toward a solution. In professional spaces, many argue to defend their pride, protect their role, or prove their point. These arguments create noise but rarely create progress. A solution-focused argument does the opposite. It cuts through tension, redirects attention to what matters, and positions you as someone who brings value instead of conflict.

A solution-focused mindset begins with intention. Before you speak, you must ask yourself a simple question: What outcome am I aiming for? Without this clarity, your words scatter. With it, your message becomes forward moving. You stop fighting the individual in front of you and start addressing the issue overshadowing the room.

In office politics, this approach is rare, which makes it powerful. Leaders notice the person who presents problems in a way that naturally points toward resolution. When you frame your argument around a constructive path, you shift the dynamic. You become someone who thinks clearly under pressure. *Someone who moves the conversation toward progress. Someone who carries influence without raising their voice.*

A solution-focused argument also lowers resistance. People open their ears when they sense progress. You create space where others expect friction. You offer direction where others expect blame. The tone shifts, the energy calms, and your message find a smoother path to acceptance.

This approach does not hide the truth. It presents the truth with a way forward. You highlight the issue, show why it matters, and reveal the path that benefits the whole structure. When people feel that your intention is growth rather than attack, they drop their guard. This is how influence begins to take root.

Mastering solution-focused argument is mastering strategic clarity. You speak with purpose, you reduce conflict, and you guide the conversation toward outcomes that strengthen your credibility. In an environment ruled by politics, this becomes your quiet advantage. It places you among the few who not only see the problem but also carry the wisdom to lead beyond it.

Note:

> a) An argument is not won by volume but by precision—say the right words, to the right people, at the right time.
> b) Power is never given; it is taken with strategy, timing, and the right audience.
> c) The most persuasive argument is not the loudest, but the one delivered at the perfect moment, in the right place, to those who matter.
> d) If you wish to claim a seat at the table, don't just speak—understand who is listening, what they value, and why they should make space for you.

The Power of Respectful Disagreement

> When an enemy becomes a friend, they often give more than you asked for; even defending you better than your own friends. It's their way of proving loyalty and redeeming their past mistakes.

Edwin Stanton, a lawyer, was infamously known for his vitriolic opposition to Abraham Lincoln. He even questioned Lincoln's intellect and abilities, underestimating him first as a lawyer and later as a politician. Stanton once openly mocked Lincoln, calling him *"a long-armed ape"* and refusing to share a courtroom with him. He believed Lincoln was unfit for high office.

Many expected Lincoln to repay the insult or avoid Stanton altogether. Instead, he did the opposite. Despite their acrimonious history and Stanton's initial hostility, Lincoln recognizing Stanton's remarkable abilities—appointed him as Secretary of War during the Civil War. This act of humility and trust changed everything.

Stanton, once dismissive, now saw the greatness of the man he had ridiculed. He devoted himself completely to Lincoln's leadership, working tirelessly to preserve the Union. Their bond grew from mutual respect into a deep, unspoken friendship. Stanton defended Lincoln fiercely—

sometimes even against critics within Lincoln's own government. And when Lincoln was assassinated, it was Stanton who stood by his side, his voice breaking as he said, *"Now he belongs to the ages."*

That moment immortalized not just Lincoln, but the transformation of a man who once despised him. Stanton's loyalty, in the end, was stronger than that of many who had always stood by Lincoln's side. It reminds us that friendship forged from former enmity often arises from a sincere desire to redeem past wrongs and prove unwavering faithfulness.

Lincoln's greatness lay not in his authority, but in his **emotional intelligence**. He mastered the art of disagreeing without demeaning, choosing collaboration over retaliation. By appointing Stanton; the very man who once mocked him, Lincoln proved that true leadership separates pride from purpose. He understood that progress depends on inclusion, not exclusion.

Stanton, moved by such grace, turned from critic to ally, from rival to defender. To master disagreement is not to win arguments, but to win understanding; to hold conviction with humility and lead with a heart wise enough to turn opposition into loyalty.

Observance of power

Most of the time disagreement is less about interest and more about ego and security. This is where emotional intelligence acts as a double-edged sword: it can either defend your ego or dissolve it long enough to understand the other person.

In conflict, even when we sense we are wrong, pride rarely lets us admit it. We search for excuses, twist facts, or even escalate tension, just to preserve the illusion of being right. The need to protect our self-worth often outweighs the need for resolution. Yet a leader with emotional intelligence rises above this instinct. They do not seek victory over others, but harmony within the situation. Their focus is not on who wins the argument, but on what sustains progress.

In heated moments, the phrase *"You're wrong"* creates distance, not clarity. It hardens walls that could have been doors. A wiser approach is silence that listens, not silence that resents. Let your opponent speak. Hear them fully—both their logic and their fear. When they finish, acknowledge the truth in their words, even if it's small. Then, share your view gently, weaving your perspective through theirs. This act of inclusion disarms resistance; it builds trust and opens space for honest dialogue.

This kind of dialogue makes people feel respected and included. It builds trust and paves the way for a more constructive exchange; one where both sides feel heard, valued, and willing to cooperate. When you acknowledge someone's perspective, you invite them to lower their defenses and rethink their stance. What begins as opposition often transforms into understanding and sometimes, even into alliance.

Most conflicts are not battles of ideas, but battles of ego. The moment you stop trying to win, understanding finally gets a chance to speak.

Mayank Gupta and Charan Singh were assigned to manage the guests during their company's annual award ceremony—an event that typically draws around 200 to 300 attendees each year.

However, Mayank had already made other plans. He wanted to work with his female colleague, Bhavani Roy. The two had even coordinated their outfits and discussed in advance how they would welcome guests and handle VIPs, all without waiting for official approval. Unfortunately, their preemptive planning was dismissed by management. The organizing committee had issued a strict rule: men would work with men, and women with women.

The decision shattered Mayank's expectations. Still, he didn't voice any complaint and complied with the order from the higher-ups.

On the day of the event, though, his cooperation was minimal. He frequently excused himself to engage with his female colleagues, 'particularly Bhavani' leaving Charan to manage the steady stream of guests alone. This defiance overwhelmed Charan. He struggled to handle the influx of attendees while maintaining the event's flow.

Frustration eventually boiled over. Charan confronted Mayank, accusing him of neglecting his duties and prioritizing personal interactions over professional responsibilities. Mayank, already resentful of being denied his preferred arrangement, lashed back, venting his anger at both the decision-makers and the situation.

The argument intensified. Charan made it clear that pairing with Mayank hadn't been his choice either; he was simply following orders, while Mayank insisted that his disobedience wasn't personal, but born out of frustration with the management's decision. Neither wanted to back down, and the tension escalated rapidly.

Sensing the conflict, Bhavani stepped in. She didn't want the scene to worsen, especially knowing that Mayank, a close colleague bore much of the blame.

She listened quietly to both sides before taking charge. First, she calmed Mayank and acknowledged Charan's grievances, affirming that his anger was justified. Then, she gently turned the conversation toward understanding, explaining that Mayank's behavior wasn't rooted in personal animosity but in disappointment toward the management's policy.

By reframing the conflict as a reaction to perceived unfairness rather than a personal slight, Bhavani helped Charan see the situation through a more empathetic lens. The confrontation softened, replaced by a mutual understanding that the real issue lay not between them, but in the system that had set them against each other.

Thus, Charan de-escalates the situation not because he suddenly forgives Mayank, but because Bhavani's calm mediation reframes the issue. She helps Charan see the systemic roots of Mayank's behavior, while still holding Mayank accountable for his actions, a balance that allows Charan to cool down and let the conflict ease naturally.

Personal experience

In 2025, I led a team organizing our community's annual youth camp. Our responsibilities included securing funds through contributions, fundraising, and other means, as well as selecting camp leaders and ensuring the overall welfare of the campers.

Throughout this period, we held numerous meetings, often engaging in spirited discussions about resource allocation, program priorities, and logistical challenges. These conversations, while sometimes intense, reflected our shared commitment to the success of the camp. As the team leader, I frequently had to mediate conflicts, ensuring that every member felt heard and valued while keeping our focus on the collective mission.

In each conflict, I made it a point to remain impartial, showing a genuine interest in understanding both perspectives before facilitating a resolution aligned with our overarching goals. I would listen carefully to every argument, and when necessary, support one side if it best served the team's cohesion and the project's needs. My approach was never to dismiss concerns outright but to acknowledge their validity and explore their potential value, while also highlighting practical limitations.

For instance, after hearing a proposal, I would respond with something like: *"Thank you very much for that idea—it's a good one, and I understand your point about X, which is insightful. I particularly like your suggestion regarding Y, as it could strengthen our outreach strategy. However, given our limited resources, implementing X right now might divert essential funds from Z, which remains our top priority for securing camp supplies."*

I would then explain how another team member's proposal aligned better with our current constraints and how it could advance the project with the resources we had. Finally, I'd invite collaboration by asking:

"Given these factors, how do you think we can best align your excellent idea with our current budget and overall goals? We believe Mr. A's proposal is more feasible for now, but once we have more resources, we can revisit and implement your idea." (**Note:** This approach isn't fixed; it should change according to the situation.)

This approach acknowledging contributions while steering discussions toward pragmatic solutions, helped create a collaborative atmosphere even amid disagreement. The individual whose proposal couldn't be implemented understood that the issue lay not in the idea itself but in the timing and available resources. As a result, he continued to work with the team without resentment.

This methodology effectively channeled individual energies toward a common objective, mitigating internal tensions and fostering cooperation within the team. In any conflict, strive to understand their *"why"* and *"how."* This gives you a more strategic solution rather than a purely emotional reaction. Show genuine concern for their perspective; ask questions instead of making statements. In most conflicts, individuals seek validation for their views, and acknowledging their reasoning can de-escalate tension and open space for constructive dialogue.

In conflict, *statements ignite it; questions disarm the ego.* Frame your statements as questions and let your message emerge from their answers. From those answers, gently align their thoughts with your perspective. Make them feel that your idea was born from their own reasoning. When people sense ownership of an idea, they are more likely to agree, even if they initially disagreed, simply to protect their ego. This strategic approach transforms potential confrontations into collaborative problem-solving opportunities. **In this way, you can disagree with grace and guide your opponent toward a consensus that serves the collective goal.**

Don't ever try to humiliate your opponent, even when you're right. Winning an argument at the cost of someone's dignity is never a real victory—it just plants the seed for future resistance. Let them save face.

You can make your point without making them feel small. People rarely remember what you said in a disagreement, but they always remember how you made them feel.

Respecting their dignity, even in conflict, turns potential rivals into future allies. The way you handle disagreement says more about your character than your argument ever will.

In the late 1970s, the tension between Egypt and Israel felt impossible to unmap. Generations had grown up seeing the other side as a threat. Borders carried scars. Every meeting between the two nations ended in suspicion. Trust seemed unreachable.

Yet something shifted when Anwar Sadat, the President of Egypt, made a surprising choice. He decided to visit Jerusalem for a direct conversation. Many feared this decision. Many warned him that a visit to the heart of a rival nation would end in humiliation. Sadat moved forward anyway.

When he arrived, he did not speak like a man seeking triumph. He spoke with calm strength, admitting that both nations had suffered. He shared hopes for a future that did not revolve around fear. Menachem Begin, the Prime Minister of Israel, listened. He expected accusation or pressure. Instead, he heard honesty, sorrow, and clarity.

Their first meeting did not erase the past. They disagreed on many points. Yet the tone changed. Sadat listened. Begin listened. They disagreed with respect. Each saw the other as a human being, not a symbol of danger. Gradually, the hostility lost its grip.

Talks continued for months. Disagreements remained sharp, yet both leaders kept speaking with dignity. This opened a path that once seemed impossible. They signed a treaty that changed the region's future. The world watched two former enemies stand together, not as perfect friends, but as partners willing to shape a different tomorrow.

Their story shows that strength lies not in forcing someone to accept a view. It lies in meeting them with a voice that refuses to insult or belittle. A voice that stands firm without hostility. A voice that chooses understanding over pride.

Respectful disagreement has that kind of power. It can turn suspicion into conversation, conversation into cooperation, cooperation into alignment. When we listen fully, question gently, then state our truth with steadiness, even an enemy can find a reason to stand beside us.

A smile can hide the deepest betrayal.

Judas Iscariot, one of the twelve apostles of Jesus Christ, is forever infamous for his betrayal—a single act that altered the course of history. As one of Jesus' closest followers, Judas was entrusted with managing the group's finances. Yet beneath the surface, he allowed greed to take root, secretly pilfering from the common purse. When the religious leaders set their sights on Jesus, Judas saw an opportunity for profit, betraying his Messiah for a mere thirty pieces of silver. Under the cover of night, he led the high priest's soldiers to the Garden of Gethsemane, where Jesus and His disciples were deep in prayer. There, in a moment steeped in deception, Judas identified Jesus with a kiss—a gesture of friendship twisted into an act of betrayal.

Judas began following Jesus out of genuine devotion. Like the other apostles, he was drawn to the message of salvation and the promise of a new kingdom. Betraying Jesus was never his original intent, but over time, his love for money, his greed consumed him. No one would have expected the loyal apostle, the trusted treasurer, to turn against the very Messiah he had pledged to follow. Yet this is the tragic irony of Judas' story: a life that began with promise ended in the deepest personal and spiritual ruin.

One can never be certain about the future. Even those closest to us can turn against us when selfish desires take root. God Himself was betrayed by one of His own chosen disciples.

As it is written in the Bible, *"There is no one righteous, not even one"*—a truth that includes even those we trust the most. Indeed, the devil's greatest weapon is often the one closest to you.

> *(Perhaps Judas' betrayal of Jesus was another lesson God intended to teach; even through the most painful of experiences revealing the depths of human nature and the power of temptation. Though God knows all things, He allowed it to happen so that we might learn from it.)*

Perspective shift

His trusted general, Akechi Mitsuhide, betrayed the famous Japanese warlord Oda Nobunaga. Nobunaga had unified much of Japan under his rule, but in 1582, while attending a tea ceremony, Mitsuhide and his men launched a surprise attack on Nobunaga's castle. Faced with capture, the great warlord chose to commit suicide rather than surrender. Thus, the man who had conquered much of Japan through his military genius was ultimately undone by the treachery of one of his most trusted subordinates.

The greatest warlord who could not be defeated on the battlefield fell not to an opposing force, but to someone within his own ranks: a man he had entrusted with power. Nobunaga had placed his faith in Mitsuhide, only to have that trust brutally betrayed.

Mitsuhide had been a loyal subordinate, entrusted with great authority and responsibility. No one could have imagined that he would turn against Nobunaga, the very man who had elevated him to such prominence. Yet the lure of power and ambition proved too strong, leading Mitsuhide to commit the ultimate act of betrayal.

Loyalty, trust, and the unimaginable acts of betrayal are all too common in the annals of history. Even the mightiest, wisest, and most brilliant of rulers become vulnerable when those closest to them break their trust.

Julius Caesar, the Roman dictator, was betrayed by his close ally Brutus, who led a conspiracy to assassinate him. Macbeth, a capable and ambitious general, was led astray by his wife's manipulations and the prophecies of witches, ultimately bringing about his downfall. King Arthur, the legendary British ruler, was betrayed by his trusted knight Lancelot, who had an affair with Guinevere, Arthur's queen. Shah Jahan, the Mughal emperor who built the Taj Mahal, was imprisoned by his own son Aurangzeb, who seized power for himself.

In all these cases, the betrayal came not from distant enemies, but from those who had been entrusted with power and privilege.

A mighty vessel, forged to brave the storm,
Was felled not by the tempest's raging might,
But by the silent gnawing, small yet warm,
Of rats within, who feasted in the night.

A leader; even the strongest in history often falls not at the hands of enemies, but by those closest to them. Their downfall comes not through mighty adversaries, but through the silent, insidious betrayal of those who once stood by their side. Like rats gnawing at a ship from within, the greatest destruction often arises unseen—from those we least expect.

And yet, this truth extends far beyond kings and generals. In every life, trust is both a strength and a risk. We open our hearts, believing in loyalty, only to discover that even the most faithful can be swayed by the lure of power, greed, or ambition. The ultimate betrayal lies in that moment when trust collapses; when those we once leaned on for strength turn against us, driven by selfish desire.

For betrayal is rarely loud; it moves in silent, wearing the face of friendship and the voice of reassurance. Our enemies are not always the ones who stand before us in defiance, but those who linger in the shadows, hidden behind masks of loyalty and affection. Be wise and discerning, for even a friend's smile can conceal the deepest wound.

Corporate experience

2024: In mid-November, Nayana was forced to resign from her managerial position at a major telecommunications company after the managing director discovered that she planned to leave for a competitor offering a much higher salary early the next year. She was shocked and disappointed when she received the termination email—utterly bewildered. *Why did this happen? How did the director find out about my plans?* Apart from her close colleague Rizwan, she hadn't shared her intentions with anyone. Yet, the office grapevine seemed to have worked its magic.

Nayana had been a loyal employee of the company for six years and had known Rizwan for more than three. She trusted him as a good friend, confiding in him about her future plans, never imagining he would turn on her. But how could her private words have reached the director when she had only shared them with Rizwan?

When a secret conversation between you and a friend is revealed, how do you think it happens?

The friends we least expect to betray us are often the ones who stab us in the back when we least see it coming. We may never know how many "Rizwans" lurk in our midst, waiting to seize an opportunity to satisfy their greed or ambition, even at the cost of a trusted friendship. Be cautious and discerning; not everyone who smiles at you is your ally. Don't let the mask of friendship blind you to the truth behind someone's intentions. In the end, the only path to true security and success is to rely on yourself; on your abilities, discipline, and discernment, rather than the fickle loyalty of others.

How many times have we seen a trusted friend reveal their true colours only when it serves their interests?

Avoid trusting too quickly or being naive about the motives of those around you. Maintain healthy boundaries; be willing to make difficult choices when you sense duplicity, and pay attention to inconsistent behavior or excessive self-interest. The people closest to us know both our strengths and our weaknesses, and thus possess the greatest power to harm us if their loyalties become corrupted by greed or selfish desire.

A friend feels loyal when life stays simple, yet once power enters the picture; true character steps forward, revealing who values you and who values gain.

Betrayed by Loved One

Joti was shattered when she discovered that her boyfriend of two years had been cheating on her with another woman. She had trusted him completely, and the two had shared a live-in relationship in Delhi. A working professional, Joti was also the breadwinner in their relationship. Handling foreign clients, she often worked late into the night. Unbeknownst to her, while she was away at work, her boyfriend would bring the other woman home and spend the night with her.

One evening, Joti returned earlier than usual because she was feeling unwell. To her horror, she found the two in a compromising position. Distraught and heartbroken, she realized that the man she had loved and trusted the most had betrayed her in the worst possible way. Without hesitation, she ended the relationship. Yet the trauma of his betrayal lingered—she had given so much of herself, only to be left with pain.

Joti left her family and the safety of home to live with the man she believed was her future. Every choice she made, every sacrifice she carried, was built on trust and hope. She shared her life with him; her space, her work, her dreams, and her vulnerabilities without holding anything back. But the trust she offered so freely became the very thing that left her exposed.

Despite her devotion, she was met with betrayal. She had given him her emotions, her loyalty, and her heart, only to discover they were taken for granted and twisted against her. The life she had imagined together fell apart, and with it, the faith she had placed in someone she believed would never hurt her. Her love had made her vulnerable, and the wound it left ran deeper than any loss of comfort or possessions—she was not merely betrayed by a man, but by the very faith she had placed in love itself.

As an old Naga folk song whispers:

> *The dog we feed to guard us bites the hand that feeds.*
> *The child we cradle in love grows thorns to pierce the hands that held them dear.*
> *The wife who shares our bed shares it with another, while we chase the wild winds.*

This folk song may belong to another culture, yet its message is universal. A husband returns from the hunt or from war, only to find his wife in the arms of another man. He battles enemies to protect his home, only to be wounded by treachery from within. As the lyrics lament, even the most loyal of beasts may turn and bite the hand that feeds it. Such is the tragic nature of betrayal.

Be cautious in love, for even the most ardent passion can wither under the weight of human weakness, greed, and selfishness. When we give our emotions to someone, we hand them the power to wound us. To guard against betrayal, protect your heart with wisdom—the only true defense is not to surrender it completely. Love deeply, but always maintain an inner citadel that cannot be breached, for the heart is both a gift and a risk.

Chapter note:

- ♠ The devil's greatest weapon is often the one closest to you.
- ♠ When we give our heart completely to another, we place ourselves at their mercy.
- ♠ Lover and friends can become foes in the blink of an eye when the temptation of power, money, or status becomes too great.
- ♠ Never give all your heart, for love is a fragile bond that can shatter in an instant.

Personal experience:

When I published my first book, I unintentionally released a rough draft instead of the final version. At the time, I had no idea something had gone wrong. Eager for honest feedback, I gave an author copy to a close friend, trusting him to provide constructive criticism. Instead, he quietly spread negative remarks about my work, and when I asked for his opinion, he simply said it was **"great."**

For weeks, I didn't notice anything unusual, preoccupied as I was with other work. Then, readers began pointing out flaws, and whispers about the book's quality reached me. That's when I realized the truth—I had published the wrong draft. The sting of the mistake was compounded by the betrayal of someone I had trusted, someone I thought would guide me rather than exploit my vulnerability.

The experience left me with an uncomfortable lesson: trust is delicate, and not everyone who stands close to you truly has your best interests at heart. Vulnerability is necessary for growth, but it also exposes us to harm. The key is learning how to share it wisely, to protect your heart without closing it entirely. Some lessons, as painful as they are, teach us not only about others, but about how carefully we must choose who to let in.

The Hidden Hand behind Power

***Victory belongs not to the strongest nor the cleverest, but to those who know when and where to fight.*

On the Discovery Channel, a lion stalks a monkey perched on a tree branch. The monkey responds with open-mouth stares and head bobs; typical threat displays before attempting to retreat beyond the lion's reach. But the lion anticipates the movement and pounces, bringing the chase to a swift and violent end. Its superior strength and speed easily overpower the monkey's evasive manoeuvres.

Later, after finishing its meal, the lion releases a low growl; signalling satiation and territorial assertion, both common post-feeding behaviours among apex predators—before heading to the riverside for a drink. Unaware of the lurking danger beneath the murky water, it approaches the edge, where a crocodile lies in wait, perfectly camouflaged and ready to strike.

Suddenly, the water erupts. The crocodile lunges, snapping its powerful jaws around the lion's muzzle in a brutal display of raw predatory instinct. The struggle is fierce but brief; the crocodile drags the feline into the depths, and the grim aquatic battle ends with its decisive victory.

The lion, king of the jungle, is reduced to nothing more than a meal for the crocodile; the monkey, famed for its agility and intelligence, is reduced to a meal for the lion. In nature, power is always relative, and every predator eventually meets another force greater than itself. Whether on land or in water, survival is never guaranteed; it belongs not to the strongest or the cleverest alone, but to those who adapt, endure, and choose their battles wisely.

The lion may reign over the savanna, but it holds no dominion beneath the sea, just as the sea cannot command the land. Every creature, regardless of its status, possesses its own strengths and weaknesses, and those who recognize and harness them are the ones who truly maximize their chances of survival.

Interpretation

In politics, there are always dominant figures (the lions) and agile survivors (the monkeys). The lion represents those who rely on brute strength, authority, or status, while the monkey embodies intelligence, wit, and adaptability. Both approaches have value, but neither is foolproof. The monkey's agility delays defeat but cannot fully outmatch the lion's power; just as clever tactics cannot always overcome entrenched authority. Similarly, the lion's reliance on raw power proves inadequate when confronted by the crocodile. This shows that no one is powerful in every arena. Even the strongest leaders are vulnerable when forced out of their comfort zones. Strength and cleverness are not enough. **Context, adaptability, and knowing when and how to fight matter most.** Just as survival in the wild depends on choosing the right battles and terrains, navigating office politics requires strategic awareness of your strengths, recognition of others' advantages, and the wisdom to fight only when the odds favor you.

From the Pages of History

Paoshi was not only the name of a man, but also a symbol of the perfect warrior in ancient Naga folklore. Wherever he went, his very presence was enough to inspire both fear and respect. Neighboring villages and tribes trembled at his reputation. One old folk song tells of him: *"Even the birds of the air ceased their singing when Paoshi was near. The wind itself grew colder in his presence, and enemies quaked at the mere mention of his name. A mighty headhunter—while ordinary hunters ventured fearlessly into enemy lands, they would cower like mice when Paoshi was on the warpath."*

He was challenged by no one; his prowess in battle was legendary, and his tactics unmatched. In one raid, Paoshi slew a man; beheading him and carrying the head as a trophy, unaware that the fallen warrior was the father of a young boy hiding nearby. The child, forced to witness both his father's death and the devastation of his village, wept in despair. Struck by pity at the sight of the orphan, Paoshi took the boy under his wing, intending to raise him as his own son.

Yet within the boy grew a burning desire for vengeance. He waited patiently for the moment to strike against the man who had orphaned him. One day, as Paoshi lay drunk and asleep, the boy seized his chance. He drove a dagger into Paoshi's chest and severed his head to avenge his father's death. Thus Paoshi—the warrior of immense strength and legendary power was not brought down by a rival in open battle, but by the hidden hand of vengeance.

The boy, who seemed weak and defenceless, changed the course of history; not by brute force or open confrontation, but through patience, cunning, and an intimate understanding of his adversary's vulnerabilities.

Observance of power

In the game of politics, no one holds all the cards; nor is there anyone who holds none. Everyone, even the seemingly weakest, possesses some leverage that can be exploited under the right circumstances. Politics is like a chess match where each piece, regardless of its perceived value, can contribute to the strategic objective through calculated moves and anticipation of an opponent's weaknesses. Understand that the most effective political actors are those who can identify the vulnerabilities of others while simultaneously concealing their own. Read the moves of your opponents as if they were laid bare on a chessboard, and formulate your strategy based on their revealed intentions and hidden motivations, for power dynamics often involve a subtle interplay of overt actions and concealed agendas.

If needed, grant them a measure of power to psychologically disarm them, allowing them to believe they are gaining influence while you quietly prepare for an opportune countermove. Your aim is to win, not to shield every piece from sacrifice. A cunning chess player often gives up minor pieces to gain a strategic advantage or to expose critical weaknesses in an opponent's defense, ultimately leading to victory. Like chess, political strategy demands calculated sacrifices to achieve greater objectives. Offer them the illusion of control, let their true inclinations and vulnerabilities surface, and then exploit those insights; turning their perceived gains into the very means of their downfall.

> *A dominant force lasts only until it steps into the one place where its power holds no meaning.*

The Battle of Isandlwana (1879)

In 1879, during the Anglo-Zulu War, the British army entered Zululand with absolute confidence. They were one of the most dominant military forces in the world, equipped with rifles, artillery, and a long history of victory. Their commanders believed that no local force could challenge them. In their minds, they were the lions of the conflict.

Yet that confidence became their blind spot. The British set up camp at Isandlwana without proper defenses. They split their troops, underestimated the Zulu army's mobility, and assumed their firepower would compensate for every mistake. What they failed to see was that they had walked into terrain they did not understand. Their strength on open European-style battlefields did not automatically make them strong on the African plains.

The Zulu army moved with speed, coordination, and a deep understanding of their land. They approached in their signature "horns of the buffalo" formation, surrounding the British from multiple sides. When the battle began, the British lines could not adapt fast enough. Their ammunition supply faltered, their formations broke apart, and their firepower advantage vanished in the chaos.

Within hours, a force that believed itself untouchable was overwhelmed by opponents they had dismissed as inferior.

The British were not defeated because they lacked strength, but because they underestimate their opponent. They stepped into a zone where their advantage held little meaning, much like a lion approaching water without noticing a crocodile waiting beneath the surface.

The core idea of Isandlwana message is:

- *Power is never absolute.*
- *Strength only works in the right environment.*
- *Underestimating others creates openings for your own downfall.*
- *Even a dominant force collapses when pushed out of its familiar ground.*

The Zulu victory did not come from greater weapons or superior global power. It came from awareness, adaptability, and exploiting the exact vulnerabilities the British ignored.

Just as the lion dominates the plains but loses near the river, the British dominated traditional battlefields but lost at Isandlwana when they entered terrain that favored someone else. The outcome was a reminder that in any arena; political, military, or personal, no one is strong everywhere. Those who understand their environment, recognize the strengths of others, and strike at the right moment often shift the entire balance of power.

Bonus

The power of choosing the right words

Every word is powerful when it is placed in the right place, but it is of no use when it is used incorrectly or thoughtlessly.

Apple: It's the name of a fruit.
Eppal: It has no meaning.

Just like *"apple"* and *"eppal,"* your words can change the course of your story, whether powerful or worthless.

Words can heal, and words can wound.
A sentence spoken with kindness can open a heart; the same sentence, twisted with sarcasm, can close a door forever.

Words can build bridges, or they can burn them.
They can invite trust, or they can plant suspicion.

Think of history; wars have begun with a phrase, and peace has been signed with a word.
Think of your own life; one *"yes"* may have changed your destiny, and one careless *"no"* may have closed an opportunity forever.

Never underestimate the weight of what you say.
Your tongue may be small, but it carries the power to lift a soul or crush it.

So,

Before you speak, pause.
Before you write, reflect.
Before you respond, choose.

Because words are not just sounds or letters, they are seeds.
And every seed you plant will one day bear fruit: sweet or bitter, depending on the care with which you chose it.

Choose wisely; the story of your life is written, word by word.

Lie to Shield Your Truth

When the truth can get you killed, a lie is no longer a weakness, it becomes your strongest armour.

In the pursuit of power, the boundary between truth and deception is never as clear as we imagine. There are moments when exposing your truth can cost you everything, and in such moments, a well-placed lie is not betrayal—it is noble-lie.

Plato, in *The Republic*, justified the **"noble lie"**—a carefully crafted deception that preserved order and strengthened the state. It wasn't truth that built empires, but the wisdom to know when truth should be spoken, and when it should be shielded.

Sun Zian was a prime minister of ancient China, tasked with preserving the peace and stability of the realm. During the invasion of a rival kingdom, the queen feigned illness and, within days, passed away. One of the queen guards carried this report, which was meant to be delivered to the king at the border, where he was leading his troops. At that time, however, the king was already engaged in a decisive battle. In his absence, Sun Zian often assumed command of the holding camp. Upon receiving the guard's grim news, Sun Zian chose to conceal the queen's death from the king, recognizing that such a revelation could gravely undermine morale and strategic focus during a pivotal military engagement.

Without the king's consent, he summoned the ministers and lords to collectively mourn the queen, orchestrating a public display of grief that both honored her memory and projected an image of stability and continuity to the populace. From that moment on, under Sun Zian's guidance, the ministers themselves helped sustain the deception—keeping the lie alive for years—until the king finally returned.

When the king returned from the war, Sun Zian; one of his most trusted and favored ministers, entered the royal chambers. There, he removed his ceremonial robes, ministerial scepter, and cap, and prostrated himself before his monarch to accept the penalty for his audacious deception. Clothed only in white, he bowed his head and confessed that his actions were unforgivable, insisting that all blame lay upon him alone and declaring his willingness to accept whatever punishment the king might decree.

Upon hearing this, the king was furious and ordered his execution. Yet the gathered ministers and advisors interceded, pleading for Sun Zian's life. They argued that while his deception was grave, it had been guided by loyalty and the intent to preserve the kingdom's stability during a critical moment. All the ministers begged the king to reconsider, and at last, moved by their counsel and remembering Sun Zian's long record of faithful service, the king relented. Still, by imperial law, Sun Zian was stripped of his rank and he was outcast from the city.

Yet, only a few years later, the king reinstated him to his former position, restoring both his honor and his place at the heart of the court.

> *Power is not only in speaking the truth; it is in knowing when the truth must wait.*

Interpretation

Sun Zian's deception was never for himself, it was for the life of a kingdom. His lie became a shield, not against enemies alone, but against despair itself. In choosing silence over truth, he was not turning away from virtue; he was bending it to serve a greater purpose. Confucian wisdom speaks of duty—duty to the family, to the ruler, to the state, and Sun Zian lived that duty even at the cost of his own honor.

Sometimes, a lie can serve loyalty in ways truth cannot. A lie becomes a strategic instrument, deployed when the unvarnished truth threatens the very foundations of societal order or the success of critical endeavors. In such cases, deception is not a moral failing but a pragmatic necessity. Yet this path is treacherous. A lie can save a crown, but it can also shatter the trust upon which that crown rests.

The art lies in knowing the measure.—**lie only to the extent you can afford.** Strategic deception can guard your truth and secure your future, but reckless lies will dig your grave faster than any truth ever could. A lie, when used wisely, is not the end of truth; it is the shield that keeps it alive.

Warning:

In the fevered days of the French Revolution, Maximilien Robespierre did not see himself as a liar. He saw himself as a guardian of virtue. France, he believed, stood on a fragile edge, surrounded by enemies within and without. Truth, in its raw form, felt too slow, too gentle for the violence of the moment. So he reshaped it.

Accusations were sharpened, suspicions amplified, facts arranged to fit the urgency of his vision. Each distortion was justified as necessity. Each lie was wrapped in the language of moral duty. To Robespierre, deception was not betrayal; it was sacrifice. He believed the Republic could be purified only if truth bent to serve the revolution's survival.

For a time, it worked. Fear became a tool. Silence became obedience. The machinery he built moved swiftly, consuming rivals and dissenters alike. Yet deception has a hunger of its own. It demands escalation. What began as selective truth soon became habitual distortion, and trust began to thin. Eventually, the crowd could no longer tell where justice ended and manipulation began. The very standards Robespierre used to condemn others were turned toward him. His words, once treated as moral law, were reexamined. His motives, once unquestioned, were placed under suspicion.

When Robespierre was arrested, there was no lie left strong enough to save him. The guillotine he had legitimized in the name of virtue awaited him without hesitation. The system he sustained through distortion did not collapse with him; it completed its logic.

Play dumb and act smart

Alicia Souza was a cartoonist; playful, mischievous, and full of tomfoolery in her work, often weaving humor and satire into her art. She would ask her peers silly questions and sometimes pretend to play the fool during gatherings. Her behavior seemed childish and unserious; no one saw her as a threat. Yet, within a year, she was suddenly promoted to assistant director.

Her playbook was simple: she knew how to hack the system by **playing the fool to slip past obstacle**s and introduce novel ideas. She would play dumb in front of colleagues who might otherwise impede her progress, and act childlike with others to extract information. Behind this mask, no one considered her a threat to their position, nor did they perceive her as capable of outmaneuvering them. This meant there was little jealousy or resistance to her rise.

Quietly, she advanced her career significantly. She understood who the gatekeepers were and how to influence them. She would flatter these gatekeepers by highlighting her achievements and, at times, by presenting her plans directly to the key holders who had the power to influence her advancement. She made it seem as though her voice was theirs, prompting the gatekeepers to assign tasks to the team. Once the team executed them, Alicia would attribute the success back to the gatekeepers.

Alicia gave them victory while keeping the recipe to herself. The gatekeepers gladly accepted the praise, but deep down they knew it was all Alicia's plan. To them, she was a valuable asset. Meanwhile, her colleagues believed the tasks originated from their superiors, since the command appeared to come from the top rather than from Alicia herself. This strategic game allowed her to win her position without ever appearing to overtly challenge or threaten her peers. By the time they understood her game, she was already too far ahead for them.

Key to power:

Power rarely belongs to the loudest voice in the room; it rests with the one who orchestrates influence from the periphery. Alicia surreptitiously employed naivety as her disguise, concealing her ambitions while subtly guiding outcomes and leveraging relationships to achieve her professional goals without overt confrontation. This covert approach allowed her to bypass direct competition and instead cultivate an environment where her contributions were recognized and rewarded, without inciting resentment or resistance from peers or superiors.

She wore the mask of naivety. By pretending to be unserious, playful, or even slightly foolish, Alicia lowered the defenses of her peers. No one felt threatened. When people dismiss you, they stop competing with you. This gave her the freedom to move quietly, without resistance, until the moment was right. This deliberate downplaying of her capabilities enabled her to gather crucial insights and build alliances unnoticed, positioning her for a strategic ascent within the organizational hierarchy. Such an approach was not luck; it was deliberate design. She mastered the art of appearing harmless while being deeply calculating. Play dumb and act smart. This is the paradox of power: those who seem least dangerous often hold the greatest advantage. By the time others uncover your game, you will already be sitting where they hoped to stand. Indeed, the subtle manipulation of perception and the strategic use of apparent weakness are among the most powerful, if hidden, methods of career advancement.

The fewer the enemies, the easier the climb to success.

Mastering the art of impression management

Why is it that the least attractive man often walks hand in hand with the most stunning woman? Or that the least deserving colleague somehow secures the promotion, and the loyal employee remains overlooked? In many corporations, *who* you impress often matters more than *what* you contribute. Blind loyalty to your work alone can easily lead you into a pitfall. To succeed in today's hyper-connected, influence-driven world, one must master the subtle and strategic art of impression management.

This dynamic is not a modern anomaly; history has long shown that influence often outshines merit. **Louis XIV's court at Versailles**: nobles who mastered the art of flattery and presence gained land, titles, and influence—while more capable administrators faded into the background. The same dynamic lives on today. In modern organizations, those skilled in impression management often win preferential treatment and career advancement, regardless of actual competence or dedication.

The spoils system of 19th-century America was another stage for the same drama. What looked like politics was, at its heart, the psychology of influence at work. Positions were handed not to the most capable, but to those whose loyalty and presence reassured those in power. Modern offices are no different. Titles and promotions often flow toward the colleague who masters the art of being seen, rather than the one who quietly sustains the work. Impression management, whether through charm, loyalty, or subtle alignment with authority, becomes the hidden currency. And so, just as at Versailles or within the spoils system, merit alone rarely decides the outcome; it is the perception of merit that often dictates career trajectories and organizational rewards.

In most families, among siblings, those who manage to impress their parents often receive preferential treatment, while the quiet one; the one who takes care of household chores, tends to be overlooked. The same dynamic plays out in the workplace: employees who skillfully manage their image often gain an advantage in securing promotions and rewards from their superiors, while those who focus solely on their tasks may see their contributions undervalued. This is why it is crucial to understand the strategic manipulation of perception, known as impression management or risk being overshadowed by more visible colleagues.

Promotion is rarely a measure of contribution; it is a measure of perception.

The art of argument

Argument is not the right way to convince someone; it can, however, be used to distract or mislead an opponent while you cover your tracks, especially if you are practicing deception or have been caught in a lie. This tactic is common among politicians who use rhetorical tricks to obscure facts and manipulate their opponents.

In the heat of debate, people often become less guarded and more impulsive; they will say almost anything to win, regardless of the truth. That is your opportunity to exploit their emotional state by redirecting focus or planting strategic distractions. By luring an opponent with seemingly advantageous arguments, one can induce them to abandon their initial positions, thereby creating an opening for a decisive maneuver.

Athens, 399 BCE. Socrates was brought before the court, not to be judged by proof but by persuasion. His accusers Meletus, Anytus, and Lycon played on the emotional biases of the jury instead of presenting substantive evidence. They offered no solid proof that he corrupted the youth or defied the gods; instead, they stirred suspicion and fear, shifting the trial from evidence to imagination. This approach, where emotional appeals overshadowed facts, painted Socrates as a dangerous disruptor and relied on the persuasive force of rhetoric to sway judgment. When truth could not condemn, fear was made to speak in its place.

Socrates answered with calm logic, irony, and refusal to flatter. Yet logic alone was powerless against accusations designed to inflame. In that chamber, argument was never meant to clarify—only to conceal. His composure could not pierce the veil of misdirection. And so Athens condemned its philosopher, not because he was proven guilty, but because emotion was dressed as truth. He was found guilty and sentenced to death; not by evidence, but by bias.

A lie wrapped in eloquence will sway more hearts than truth spoken plainly.

Interpretation

An argument can be a powerful tool for influencing perceptions and swaying judgment into the desired direction. It can cloud what is clear and obscure what is obvious by leveraging cognitive biases and informal fallacies inherent in human reasoning. In Socrates, how easily fear can be dressed as truth, how suspicion can outweigh evidence, and how persuasion can silence wisdom. His fate was sealed not by proof of guilt, but by the power of rhetoric to turn uncertainty into conviction.

Ever seen lawyers use such evocative language, or politicians resort to ad hominem attacks instead of addressing policy? Or have you encountered a nobleman condemned not because he was guilty, but because he appeared guilty in the eyes of the jury? In the courtroom, lawyers frequently employ rhetorical strategies and emotive language, utilizing informal fallacies and cognitive biases to shape the jury's perceptions and influence decision-making. And as a result, the ability to skillfully construct and present arguments becomes paramount for achieving favorable legal outcomes.

Truth, on its own, is not always enough. It must find listeners willing to hear it. The lawyer won the cases not necessarily because of the undeniable facts of the case, but because their rhetorical prowess enabled them to frame the narrative in a manner that resonated with the jury's predispositions. Therefore, you must understand the art of argument, whether in the office or in any context where persuasion is essential to achieve desired outcomes.

"A clever argument can turn clarity into confusion."

Argument becomes a dangerous game when you already hold the truth. Why wrestle in shadows when the light is on your side? In the politics of the office, presenting truth with evidence carries more weight than sparring with words. For argument, in most cases, is less about revealing reality and more about blurring it and redirecting your opponent away from what is clear and toward what you desire. To rely on it when truth is yours is to trade gold for glitter, clarity for confusion.

Beware of the opportunist

Not all smiles are signs of friendship; some are rehearsals for betrayal.

If you don't guard your garden, someone else will harvest the fruits; in every workplace, there's always a hand waiting to seize what you've sown. A colleague or that one person who smiles at you might be the one wearing a sheep's clothing, covertly observing to capitalize on your efforts for their own career advancement.

There's a saying: *a fake laugh the loudest at a dull joke, a fake cry harder than the bereaved, and a fake sleep snores louder than the true sleeper.* Similarly, an opportunist often approaches with feigned sincerity, offering seemingly supportive advice while quietly gathering information to exploit for personal gain. They often come with honeyed words that mask ulterior motives, probing for vulnerabilities or ways to leverage your work for their own advantage. And once you let your guard down, they waste no time turning your weakness into a tool for their advancement.

For them, you are nothing more than a fish in the pool, baited with flattery and watched with calculation; like a fisherman who lures with sweetness only to hook what he desires.

When someone approaches you with excessive praise or flattery, study their intention and motivations. Find out the reason **"WHY"** and acknowledge them, but never be off guard. They may genuinely be supportive or may have a hidden agenda; either way, you don't have to reveal your cards. Accept their praise or flattery with grace, but that is their limit, don't let their influence sway your decisions and make them cross your boundaries, or you risk becoming a victim of your own naivety.

Rosalind Franklin was a classic case of such exploitation. Her critical contributions to the discovery of the DNA double helix structure went largely uncredited during her lifetime, as her meticulous X-ray diffraction images and data were appropriated by Watson and Crick, who subsequently claimed sole credit for the breakthrough. Only much later, after her death, was her pivotal role begrudgingly acknowledged.

Perhaps, she might have seen her contributions recognized sooner had she guarded her data more carefully. Yet a single misstep; perhaps an unexpected naivety in sharing her findings allowed others to capitalize on her intellectual labour.

A key from a Friend:

It's not uncommon to find a friend betrayed by a friend; somehow, there is always a Judas in every circle. One friend, in naïve trust, bares all their vulnerabilities to someone they believe is loyal only to discover later that this trust becomes the cruelest form of betrayal.

Even the strongest person, unshaken by external threats, is often undone by the very individuals they trusted most. It is no surprise, then, that when we attach our emotions to those we cherish, we naturally feel secure and open. Yet that very openness leaves us exposed—like resting peacefully in our own home, never certain if a thief is waiting just beyond the door.

Be comfortable with your friends, open up to them, but never at the expense of your self-respect or by giving them the tools for manipulation. Boundaries in any relationship are not walls of coldness but acts of self-preservation. Only those who learn to guard this balance can sustain healthy connections, both personal and professional.

Learning the art of self-mastery

"He who conquers himself is the mightiest warrior.—Kong Qiu"

In 161 AD, Rome, the greatest empire of its time, glittered with wealth yet festered with intrigue. Betrayal, unrest, and politics stalked its halls of power. At the center of it all sat Marcus Aurelius, newly crowned emperor of Rome, who, despite his immense power, was a man devoted to Stoic principles and deeply committed to self-mastery. He retreated from the tumultuous external world through introspective reflection, aligning his actions with virtue and reason.

Each night, he turned away from the tumult of the empire and opened a small wax tablet; not to boast, not to complain, but to remind himself: *"You have power over your mind—not outside events. Realize this, and you will find strength."*

Where others lashed out, he restrained his anger. Where flattery tempted pride, he humbled himself. Where despair lingered, he anchored his spirit in reason. These private notes, later known as *Meditations*, were never written for the world—they were the daily training of a man determined to govern his own mind before governing an empire. And in doing so, Marcus Aurelius preserved Rome not only through military might, but through the subtle power of self-mastery.

The Inner Battlefield

The greatest roadblock to any endeavor is not external circumstance, but an untrained mind enslaved by its own passions. When left untamed, the mind drives us toward irrational decisions and emotional biases; like an untrained animal, it reacts impulsively to every stimulus without conscious thought or rational judgment. Ego, temper, and the hunger for validation then become its masters, seizing control over our actions.

Shangeta boardroom

During a month-end meeting, Shangeta was presenting her performance when one of her colleagues interrupted her—not once, but twice. Unable to control her temper, she lost track of her presentation and lashed out in anger. True, the colleague was wrong, and he fell silent. But the damage was done. Shangeta was now seen as short-tempered in the office. The key decision-maker, though impressed by her results, hesitated over her promotion, fearing her temperament might jeopardize the team.

She became stagnant in her career not because she lacked competence, but because her emotional reactivity compromised her professional advancement. What if she had followed the rules of Marcus Aurelius and not reacted impulsively? She could have acknowledged the interruption with a calm, assertive statement, maintaining control of her presentation and demonstrating emotional intelligence. She would not only be seen as competent but also as composed and capable of handling workplace challenges, which would greatly help her professional advancement.

In pursuit of power, one must learn to control one's Ego, temper, and emotions; this internal discipline is a cornerstone for achieving any form of desire. Once you have the capacity to master these inner forces, your decisions become rational and sustainable, unclouded by transient emotional states or any other external influence.

The Wisdom of Sun Tzu

Centuries before Marcus, Sun Tzu, author of *The Art of War*, wrote a line that has outlived every battlefield:

"If you know the enemy and know yourself, you need not fear the result of a hundred battles."

Most people remember the **"enemy"** part, but Sun Tzu began with the harder half: *know yourself.*

For Sun Tzu, battles were not won by armies alone but by the mind of the commander. A general might command thousands, yet if he could not master fear, pride, or impatience, he had already lost. He warned that battles were lost not on the field but within; the general who rushed in anger, who hesitated in doubt, or who longed for glory at the wrong time doomed his men before a single arrow flew.

What Sun Tzu taught was not just strategy, but self-discipline: the ability to stay still while others panic, to wait while others rush, to act when the moment is right, not when ego demands it.

The Timeless Lesson

In office politics, the fiercest battles are not fought across the table but within the mind. Pride wants recognition, anger seeks revenge, fear craves security, yet the one who masters these forces always wins the unseen war.

Marcus Aurelius survived betrayal not by crushing his enemies, but by mastering himself. Shangeta's career faltered not from lack of skill, but from a moment of unchecked temper. Sun Tzu warned that wars are lost long before the first clash—when a leader is undone by his own impatience or ego. The lesson is the same across centuries: the greatest victories are won in private, long before they are seen in public.

In every workplace conflict, the real opponent is not your colleague but your own reaction. Stay calm when others lose control, and you'll hold the subtle power that politics cannot shake.

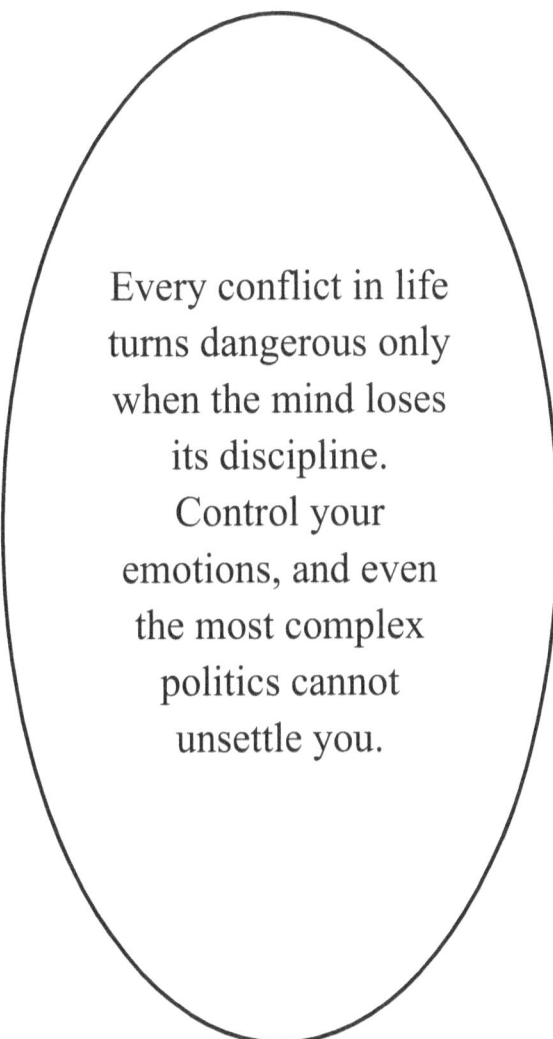

Every conflict in life turns dangerous only when the mind loses its discipline. Control your emotions, and even the most complex politics cannot unsettle you.

The art of controlling your enemy

Torata was known for his infamous behavior, cunning, and manipulative tactics, often leveraging his dominant position to neutralize potential threats within his own sphere of influence. He frequently portrayed himself as deeply invested in the group's interests, but whenever members challenged his authority, he would shift the narrative—casting himself as the victim of their supposed aggression. Because of his toxic patterns, people don't want to work with him.

Unaware of his behavior, his senior permitted him to lead the newly launched project. While it was a great opportunity for him, for the team it quickly became a foreseeable nightmare. Since the directive came from a senior, they had no choice but to follow his lead. As expected, Torata's leadership style soon resulted in significant dysfunction and declining morale, as he continued to exhibit controlling tendencies and resisted delegating authority to competent subordinates who might challenge his dominance. Many team members experienced heightened stress, anxiety, and burnout under his toxic leadership, which fostered a hostile work environment. Eventually, they began voicing their complaints to the superior, even risking their jobs with the threat of resignation if Torata was not removed from his role as team leader.

At this critical juncture, Marina, one of the team members, rose to the occasion and assumed a leadership role. During the meeting, she skillfully articulated the team's grievances while also acknowledging Torata's contributions, subtly reframing the situation to address the underlying power dynamics without directly confronting his toxic behavior. Her diplomatic approach stood out and was greatly admired by the superior, who consequently decided to retain Marina as a key project lead—shifting authority away from Torata while ensuring project continuity.

From the moment Marina took charge, everything changed; work became more efficient and collaborative, with a marked improvement in team cohesion and productivity. This was not only due to her effective leadership style but also because her approach fostered a healthier environment. Meanwhile, the team had already split into two factions; one aligned with Torata, the other with the rest of the members. While they were busy watching their rivals, they had little time to find fault with Marina. Even when her decisions were less than optimal, the team would still rally behind her—if only to prove Torata wrong. Ironically, Torata himself also supported Marina's decisions, but for the opposite reason: he wanted to show his superior that he had been right all along. Thus, with relatively little effort from Marina, both sides inadvertently contributed to the project's success. And while the factions competed for supremacy, it was Marina who received the credit for leading the team and delivering the results.

> *Sometimes the smartest way to defeat an enemy is not by clashing with them directly, but by allowing their own weight to bring them down.*

Interpretation

Torata's downfall came not because Marina directly opposed him, but because she redirected the battlefield. She didn't waste energy confronting his toxic behaviour; she acknowledged his presence, reframed the team's frustrations, and positioned herself as the solution. The irony was that even Torata, in his attempt to prove himself right, ended up strengthening her position.

This is the essence of controlling your enemy:

- **Turn conflict into leverage**: Marina used the team's division to create unity around herself.
- **Let ego be their trap**: Torata's need to appear right blinded him into supporting the very leader who replaced him.
- **Shift power without confrontation**: instead of attacking him, Marina worked with perception, earning authority in the eyes of the superior.

In the realm of politics, you must first understand the chessboard of the game you are playing and strategically position your pieces to gain an advantage. Those who study the board with patience often claim victory before others even notice the momentum turning. Subtle moves today can create openings that transform your future standing. Likewise, political actors must skillfully apply these principles to navigate complex power dynamics—often by redirecting adversarial energy for their own advancement rather than engaging in direct, costly confrontations. Master these strategies, and you can control the game.

Troy's downfall came not by force, but by its own embrace of deception. The clever hand needs no sword when pride carries the blade.

The Trojan horse

For ten long years the Greeks had battered the walls of Troy, yet the city stood unbroken. No sword, no fire, no siege could break it. Exhaustion weighed on both sides, but instead of force, the Greeks chose guile. One morning, the Trojans awoke to silence; the Greek ships were gone, and in their place stood a towering wooden horse at the city gates. Debate raged inside Troy: was it a sacred offering, or a trap? In their pride, they chose to see it as a gift of surrender, a monument to their victory. They dragged the horse within their walls, feasting late into the night.

But when darkness settled and Troy slept in celebration, the horse stirred. Hidden inside were Greek soldiers, waiting in silence. They slipped out, opened the gates, and signaled their fleet; which had only pretended to leave. Before dawn, the Greek army flooded into Troy. A city that had resisted ten years of siege crumbled in one night —not to strength, but to deception.

The unbreakable wall of Troy was exchanged for a cunning strategem that turned the Trojans' celebration into their downfall. It is like a pawn sacrificed to secure a queen in chess, where a minor loss leads to a decisive advantage. They presented the Trojan Horse as a symbol of peace or defeat, luring the enemy into a false sense of security, and in return, they were able to infiltrate the city and achieve a decisive victory.

Key to power

Flatter them with something that you can afford in order to hide the bigger picture of your true intentions, much like the Greek strategy of presenting the seemingly innocuous Trojan Horse to achieve a covert infiltration. Or, in other words, let your opponent work for you, like Torata inadvertently supported Marina, where you offer a seemingly beneficial concession that conceals a greater strategic objective; ultimately, their actions are to serve your own ends.

In the art of controlling your enemy, your aim is to make your opponent believe they are achieving their objectives while, in reality, they are merely facilitating your agenda—make the enemy focus on a constructed surface reality while your main move goes unnoticed, much like the Trojans' preoccupation with the wooden horse while the true threat lurked unseen within its belly.

> ## **WARNING:**
>
> ***Autolycus**, the grandfather of Odysseus, was famed across Greece as a master thief and trickster, renowned for his cunning, stealth, and skill with words. He could steal without being seen, deceive without being caught, and even claim others' property as his own by clever lies. Homer and later mythographers describe him as almost magical in his ability to escape detection, earning the favor of Hermes, the god of tricksters and thieves.*
>
> *Odysseus inherited much of this cunning. From childhood, he was said to be clever, resourceful, and prone to trickery — traits that would define his later adventures in the Iliad and Odyssey. The intelligence, wit, and strategic mind of Odysseus, from the Trojan Horse deception to his numerous escapes from danger echo the legacy of Autolycus, showing that cleverness can be more powerful than brute strength.*
>
> *Yet, Autolycus' talent was not guided by justice but by self-interest; his tricks enriched him, but they left behind the quiet wreckage of stolen trust. Odysseus inherited both the gift and the burden, remembered as **"the man of many turns,"** admired for his wit, yet never fully free from the suspicion his deception inspired.*

This is the danger of cleverness untempered by ethics: it dazzles in the moment but corrodes over time. To control others for selfish ends is to wrestle against the moral fabric of the world itself. Every scheme leaves a scar, every falsehood plants a seed of ruin, and in the end the trickster often becomes ensnared by the very nets he casts.

True mastery is not in bending others to serve our hunger, but in wielding our gifts with restraint; so that cleverness becomes wisdom, and power serves something greater than pride.

> **Beware the temptation to win through false deception. Every stolen advantage carries a debt; the world never forgets to collect. Be wise enough to understand the game you are in.**

The unwritten law of office politics | 156

The Quiet Strength of Emotional Intelligence

"Even the sharpest mind can be silenced if it cannot read the room."

Cleverness is not the end of the chapter. In the game of office politics, intelligence without emotional wisdom is merely a prelude to missteps and blunders. It is like a pen with no ink, present in hand yet unable to influence the page. The downfall of the brilliant rarely comes from ignorance; it comes from the emotions they could not govern, in themselves or in others.

After Julius Caesar was assassinated in 44 BC, Rome entered a dangerous power struggle. In the wake of his death, the Republic faced uncertainty, and from this turmoil, two figures quickly rose: Mark Antony, Caesar's trusted general, and Octavian, Caesar's adopted heir.

At first, Antony held the advantage. He was older, more experienced, and a skilled speaker who could stir the emotions of the crowd. His famous funeral speech for Caesar turned public anger against the assassins—proof of his ability to move people through passion. But Antony's strength became his weakness. He often let emotions dictate his choices. He openly flaunted his power, quarreled with allies, and later tied his fate to Cleopatra, Queen of Egypt. To the Roman Senate and public, this made him appear reckless, indulgent, and un-Roman.

Octavian, by contrast, practiced restraint. He rarely raised his voice, rarely acted impulsively. Instead, he studied the mood of the Senate, the fears of the people, and the pride of his allies. He presented himself as humble, calm, and disciplined; even when planning with cold precision behind the scenes.

When conflict finally came, Octavian's steady approach won. Antony, caught between passion and pride, made poor decisions. His defeat at Actium and eventual suicide left Octavian the sole master of Rome. Octavian became Augustus, the first Emperor, remembered for stability and endurance. Antony became a cautionary tale; brilliant, but undone by his inability to master himself.

Interpretation

Mark Antony had charisma, courage, and the gift of stirring hearts, but he lacked restraint. Octavian, younger and quieter, understood what Antony did not: the ability to master one's own emotions while also perceiving and guiding the emotions of others.

The contrast between Antony and Octavian highlights the two paths leaders often face. Antony embodies the danger of letting charisma and emotion go untempered: it may inspire in the short term, but it inevitably breeds instability and mistrust. Raw intelligence, on its own, is never enough to secure lasting influence or success. Octavian, by contrast, demonstrated the subtle strength of emotional discipline—listening before acting, sensing the moods of others, and exercising restraint even when provoked.

In the workplace, the lesson is clear: those who master emotional intelligence wield a deeper, quieter form of power. They can influence without shouting, stabilize without dominating, and endure where the merely clever falter. Emotional intelligence, then, is not a *"soft skill,"* it is the very foundation of strategic survival in the complex arena of office politics

Observance of power

In most cases, we do not follow the most intelligent; instead, we often end up following someone less intellectual. In the office, it is common to see leaders or seniors who are not as intellectually gifted as others still manage to attain and maintain positions of significant influence and authority. Meanwhile, those with higher degrees or stronger intellectual capabilities often struggle to gain traction or secure a position and instead find themselves following the rules set by those less intellectual.

Such situations are not rare in office manoeuvring; Steven excels at executing his tasks as a junior analyst in a marketing firm. His intellectual prowess and analytical skills are undeniable; even his superiors often consult him for complex data analysis or strategic insights. He can anticipate market trends and identify lucrative opportunities with ease. Yet, despite his exceptional abilities, when it comes to rewards or promotions, Steven is consistently overlooked, while the very colleagues and seniors he supports reap the benefits.

Steven did the work, yet the very people he helped reaped the benefits; it was as if he planted the tree only for others to harvest the fruit. He was loyal and dedicated to his team and superiors, consistently prioritizing their needs with his intellectual contributions. However, his inability to navigate interpersonal dynamics and advocate for himself meant that his brilliance often went unacknowledged and unrewarded. With limited EQ, his colleagues and superiors took advantage of his output, leaving him like a tree whose fruits were always picked by others.

In the realm of office politics, intellectual ability alone is insufficient for career advancement; the ability to understand and manage emotions, both one's own and others', is the hidden currency of influence. It is not always the sharpest mind that rises, but the one who can read the room, navigate egos, and turn conflicts into alliances. This is the power of Emotional Intelligence. It is the skill that transforms knowledge into authority, ideas into influence, and effort into recognition. Without it, even brilliance can be silenced; with it, even modest ability can command the room. In office politics, being right is never enough; you must also be emotionally wise. Those who fail to master this art may work hard yet remain unseen, while those who do shape the narrative, steer the crowd, and harvest the fruit of power.

No One Wins Alone in the Game of Office Politics

> *Brilliance without relationships often goes nowhere. Those who link with others move farther than those who stand alone. Strength grows when people choose to stand with you.*

In the 15th century, France was a fragile kingdom. The Hundred Years' War had drained its strength, and powerful nobles often behaved more like rival kings than loyal subjects. It was into this fractured world that Louis XI stepped—thin, sharp-eyed, and endlessly calculating. He would earn the name **"the Spider King"**, not for brute strength, but for the webs of alliances he spun.

Louis understood something his rivals did not: a sword may win a battle, but relationships win kingdoms. Instead of challenging mighty dukes and lords head-on, he courted them with marriages, treaties, and promises that seemed harmless at first. Where his enemies expected armies, Louis sent words. Where they prepared for battle, he prepared a snare.

He built alliances with towns, merchants, and even common people, drawing power away from the nobility. He offered privileges to cities in exchange for loyalty, giving him money and men without lifting a blade. He befriended foreign powers when it suited him; England one year, Burgundy the next, and quietly withdrew when the balance shifted.

Nobles who underestimated him often found themselves trapped: isolated, stripped of allies, and forced into submission without Louis ever needing to storm their castles. His intelligence was not the brilliance of a warrior but of a strategist who saw the invisible threads of power. By weaving those threads, he tightened the crown's grip over France.

By the time of his death in 1483, France was no longer a kingdom teetering on the edge of collapse. It was a strong, centralized state—thanks not to endless wars, but to the cunning of a man who proved that in politics, *the mind is sharper than the sword.*

Timeless lesson

Much like Louis, success in the office rarely comes from dramatic confrontations. It is shaped in conversations, in the goodwill you nurture, and in the alliances you sustain when others are too focused on open conflict. Your ability to handle the nuanced dynamics of professional relationships determines whether your initiatives gain traction or falter amidst organizational complexities.

In search of power, knowledge is like a brain, but a brain alone cannot function in isolation; to obtain power, you need the other parts of the body to function. Similarly, in organizational politics, the acquisition of knowledge must be coupled with the strategic navigation of interpersonal and interdepartmental relationships to effectively wield influence and achieve your objectives. This includes recognizing informal power structures, identifying key stakeholders, and understanding their motivations and potential opposition to change, much like political radar.

Louis XI, despite inheriting a fiscally depleted treasury and fragmented principalities from Charles VII, unified and stabilized the kingdom by building alliances and expanding his influence through diplomacy rather than continuous military engagement. His strategies still live today. In the modern workplace, your success does not rest solely on your individual brilliance or technical skill, but on your capacity to weave a web of collaboration.

> *Knowledge gives you clarity, but alliances give you strength.*

Observance

The Byzantine Empire was never the largest empire of its time, nor always the strongest. It lived in the shadow of powerful enemies; the Persians, the Arabs, the Bulgars, and later the Turks. Yet, while others rose and fell, Byzantium endured for centuries. Its secret was not brute strength, but strategy refined into an art.

Byzantine rulers understood a truth that many leaders forget: wars are won long before the battlefield. Rather than bleed their armies in endless combat, they used *diplomacy, wealth, and cunning* to shift the balance. Gold often traveled further than swords. They paid one tribe to fight another, brokered marriages that turned enemies into relatives, and spread misinformation to weaken opponents from within.

They built a reputation for being elusive; never fully predictable, never entirely vulnerable. Their leaders preferred patience over rash action, often letting enemies exhaust themselves before stepping in at the decisive moment. The empire's very survival was proof that in politics and war alike, the clever strategist defeats the reckless warrior.

One Byzantine manual of strategy advised: *"The strongest walls are not built of stone, but of alliances and foresight."* Indeed, Byzantium's greatest victories were often invisible: enemies who never attacked because they had been bought, persuaded, or divided before the battle began.

Interpretation

Byzantium endured not because it was the strongest, but because it mastered the art of building and balancing relationships. In the same way, office politics is not a contest of solitary brilliance or raw talent. Success emerges from alliances, from knowing when to support, when to yield, and when to strengthen your position. Your ideas, no matter how sharp, falter when they stand alone. To truly gain traction, even the most brilliant concepts need the solid scaffolding of strategic alliances and supportive networks. Much like Louis XI's diplomacy or the Byzantine Empire's art of paying allies, brokering trust, and turning rivals into partners, you too must learn to weave a network of cooperation. Organizational wins are not born from one discussion or one verdict; they rise from consistent effort and smart positioning; it is the unseen groundwork of trust, goodwill, and mutual interest that decides outcomes.

The unwritten law of office politics | 166

Epilogue

Everybody desires a peaceful night, a deep and undisturbed sleep. Yet it is precisely in the hush of darkness that thieves attempt to break into a house. When intruders cross that threshold, preparation becomes essential. Defending one's home and family is not a matter of cruelty or impulse. It is a necessary response driven by survival and protection. Whatever the cost, the act itself remains defensive, not malicious.

That same reality shows up inside organizations. Politics is not a rare problem; it is built into any place where people compete for influence and control. Avoiding it is not neutrality, it is exposure. Allowing organizational politics to operate unchecked is no different from allowing a silent thief to roam freely through one's home. Avoiding politics altogether resembles leaving the doors unlocked, inviting loss without resistance.

Most people do not want to deal with politics at work. Still, pretending it does not exist does not protect anyone. If you want to safeguard your career and stay relevant, you need to understand how things actually move inside an organization. Think of a student who dislikes studying yet knows one truth. Skip the work, fail the exam, lose the future. The same logic applies here. Ignore workplace politics, you leave yourself open to decisions being made without you, about you.

Organizational politics is not a game played for ego or manipulation. It is a survival tool in any layered social system. In simple terms, a man who defends his home from intruders is not acting with bad intentions. He is responding to a threat, protecting what belongs to him.

Refusing to engage in politics does not make you virtuous; it makes you unguarded. Power still moves, whether you watch or not.

The intention of this book is not to push you into playing politics, but to equip you with the awareness needed to see how power truly works. Grasping power dynamics is no different from recognizing locks, alarms, or exits. A soldier never steps into the field untrained or unequipped. Preparation is not aggression; it is survival. Professionals face a similar reality. Without insight into unspoken rules and power structures, even competence remains vulnerable. With awareness, one safeguards position, responds with precision, and moves forward with intent.

Some phrases or acronyms are used repeatedly throughout this book. This is intentional, not an error. The repetition is designed to help you become familiar with the concepts so you can recognize and apply them easily when facing challenges in your professional life.

Equip yourself so thoroughly with the knowledge of the unwritten laws of office politics that political wolves never find an opening to prey on you or your professional interests. Let your professional standing be built so solidly that even a thief would not dare to attempt a breach. Read this book not as theory, but as readiness. Use it to sharpen awareness, harden instincts, and remove hesitation. The battlefield is already active, whether you acknowledge it or not. Power does not announce itself before it strikes. You will either learn to see the threat before it reaches you, or you will become part of someone else's strategy. There is no third option.

The battlefield of influence is never empty. Power is always moving, decisions are always being made, and interests are always competing. Even when you choose to stay silent or uninvolved, the struggle does not stop. Others continue to act, plan, and position themselves. Preparation is the only real protection. When you understand how influence works, you can defend your space, protect your work, and move with confidence. When you do not, you risk being pushed aside, overlooked, or used as part of someone else's plan. In such a space, awareness is not optional. It is survival.

www.ingramcontent.com/pod-product-compliance
Lightning Source LLC
Chambersburg PA
CBHW031630210526
45464CB00004B/1833